RACING
DINGHY
HANDLING

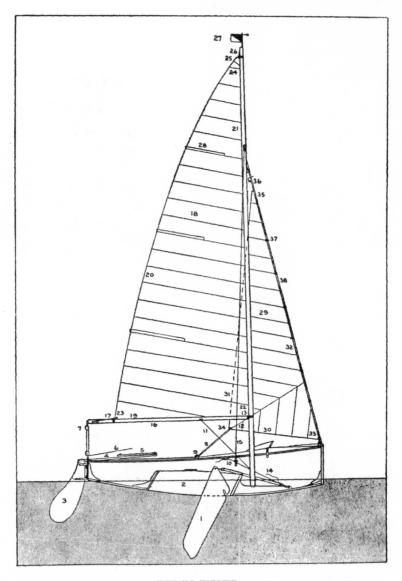

KEY TO FIGURE 1

1 Centreboard or centre-
  plate
2 Centreboard case
3 Rudder
4 Tiller
5 Tiller extension
6 Mainsheet
7 Mainsheet block
8 Foresheet
9 Foresheet fairlead
10 One of centreboard
   tackle hoists
11 Kicking strap tackle
12 Mainsail tack downhaul

13 Sliding gooseneck fitting
14 Other centreboard tackle
   hoist, leading to opposite gunwale
15 Main shroud
16 Boom
17 Mainsail clew outhaul
18 Mainsail
19 Mainsail foot
20 Mainsail leech
21 Mainsail luff
22 Mainsail tack
23 Mainsail clew
24 Mainsail head
25 Headboard

26 Main halliard
27 Racing flag
28 Batten pocket
29 Foresail
30 Foresail foot
31 Foresail leech
32 Foresail luff
33 Foresail tack
34 Foresail clew
35 Foresail head
36 Foresail halliard
37 Foresail hanks attaching
   sail to forestay
38 Forestay

RACING DINGHY HANDLING

A Complete Guide

by

IAN PROCTOR

Author of

Racing Dinghy Maintenance
Sailing: Wind and Current

ACKNOWLEDGEMENTS

I wish to offer my thanks to Mr. Gilbert Adams for permission to reproduce the photographs appearing on pages 35 and 88, and to the "Yachting World" for the photograph of the Cadet *on page 18.*

My thanks are also due to the Editor of "The Yachtsman" for permission to reprint the drawings on pages 105 and 110, which originally appeared in one of my articles in his magazine.

The Appendix on Safety Measures, added to the 1953 edition, originally appeared as an article in "Yachting World," to whose Editor I am grateful for permission to reprint.

PREFACE TO THE FIRST EDITION

Dinghy racing is one of the newest of outdoor sports. It is true that dinghies have been raced in great numbers for many years, but it was the advent in the between-war years of the light, extremely fast boat, which would plane, that accelerated the development of dinghy racing into the national sport which it is today.

The 14-*foot International* class was the beginning and some exponents of the art of racing these boats achieved almost world fame. Then followed the equally exciting but less expensive *National* 12-*footer* in 1936, and the post-war *Merlins, Fireflies, Swordfish* and *Cadets*—all first-class performers and all helping to popularize one of the finest sports ever devised.

The racing of such dinghies is an art which has now become specialized, whilst the craft themselves demand techniques of handling and maintenance which are not encountered in other sailing boats of less lively temperament. The lure of racing dinghies can seldom be resisted once it has been sampled and it seems to satisfy both the young and the older. It is not unknown for people to take up racing in these tiny temptresses at the age of sixty and to continue to sail in them for a number of years, whilst their fascination is no less difficult for children to resist. There is something thrilling and spectacular in the excitement of fifty or more boats charging across a starting line amidst a flurry of spray, or planing at a speed of perhaps twelve knots. These are the supreme moments, but for the more experienced there is equal scope for skill and no less interest in the slow progress of a fleet becalmed. There is also a fascination in the little boats themselves, each a masterpiece of craftsmanship and each requiring the care and attention of her owner. No wonder dinghy racing amounts almost to a passion among its thousands of devoted followers and is attracting newcomers in ever-increasing numbers.

A new sport needs a new book, and hence the present work has been written in the hope that it will provide the beginner with a sound introduction to modern dinghy handling, for it is upon the foundation of good handling that race-winning skill is built. The book aims to give those who are hovering on the brink of decision the information and confidence they need before entering the sport. It is hoped also that much of the contents will be of service to others of more experience, though no attempt has been made to deal with racing tactics or any aspect of sailing other than the proper handling and management of the dinghy under all conditions.

The book is arranged to describe to the beginner firstly the best-known and most widely used dinghy classes, secondly what he needs to know when crewing with an experienced skipper, and thirdly the art of helming. Two chapters are also provided on elementary dinghy maintenance, and appendices have been added explaining how to join a club and giving a list of some of the principal dinghy racing clubs. Though dealing specifically with only the best-known dinghy classes, much of what is written applies equally to the host of local one-design classes which flourish at the present time.

If this book is one of the means of getting more people afloat in dinghies, then it will have achieved its purpose.

1948.

PREFACE TO THE FOURTH EDITION

THE sport of dinghy sailing has progressed and increased in popularity in a remarkable manner in the few years since the first edition of this book was written. Fortunately several calls for new editions of Racing Dinghy Handling have enabled the text and illustrations to be kept up to date with the latest techniques and developments. In this present fourth edition the chapter on the principal dinghy classes has been completely re-written, but even so there are new classes looming over the horizon and they may well demand inclusion later on.

I am indeed grateful to the many who have been kind enough to say or write to me that this book has helped them to learn how to handle their boats and get more fun from them. I am very conscious of the fact that a book on sailing can at the best of times be no more than a mere guide—you've got to get out on the water and actually sail and learn by experience. No one has so far told me that they did as directed in this book and ended up gulping water alongside their upturned boat—so that, although this has no doubt happened from time to time, I'm happy to say that so far I have been exonerated from blame.

1955.

CONTENTS

Chapter   *Page*

I   DINGHY CLASSES. National 12-footers — International 14-footers — Fireflies — Merlin-Rockets — Hornets — Cadets — Swordfish — National 18's — Redwings — G.P. 14's — Graduates —Fleetwinds—Kestrels—New Classes—Local Classes—Other Classes..   9

II   BUYING A BOAT. Choice of class — Cost — Moorings or stowage ashore—Portability—What will you use her for?—Local sailing conditions—Choosing the design or build—Finding a second-hand boat—Racing records—Condition—Defects   ..   24

III   CREWING (1)—RIGGING AND JOBS ASHORE. Importance of good crewing—What to wear—Rigging—Shrouds and forestay—Sails—Battens—The mainsheet—Hoisting sails—The kicking strap—Check of gear—Time check—Starting signals   ..   31

IV   CREWING (2) — GETTING AFLOAT AND ASHORE. Moving dinghies — Lifting a dinghy — Trolleys — Launching — Getting aboard—Leaving and approaching the shore—Getting the dinghy ashore—Unrigging—Care of sails—Hosing down and leathering off—Stowing—Sharing the duties with skipper   ..   41

V   CREWING (3)—MAINLY ON SAIL TRIMMING. Psychological survey—Points of sailing—Tacking—Starboard tack, right of way—Action of sails to windward—Real and apparent wind— Trim—The flow of sails—Effects of light weather—Technique to windward—Effects of rough water—Goosewinging the foresail— Spinnakers—Changing tack—Sliding seats—Trapezes   48

VI   CREWING (4) — WEIGHT DISTRIBUTION, BALANCE AND KICKING STRAPS. Effects of heeling—Maintaining equilibrium—Sitting out—Fore and aft trim—Light weather— Functions of a centreboard—Leeway—Lateral resistance—Centre of effort—Balance—Weather helm—Centreboard off the wind— Light airs—Kicking straps   60

VII   CREWING (5)—HEAVY AND LIGHT WEATHER TASKS. Heavy weather technique—Preventing a capsize—Running and gybing in a strong wind—Planing—Reefing—Righting a capsize— A swamped dinghy—Towing—Anchoring—Sum-up   68

VIII   HELMING (1) — HELMSMAN'S RESPONSIBILITIES. Understanding of crew's tasks—Explaining aims—Fitting centreboards—Stepping masts—Tensioning sails—Useful and essential gear—Studying the course—Leaving and approaching the shore   76

7

CONTENTS

Chapter   *Page*

IX HELMING (2) — SAIL TRIMMING AND STEERING.
Trim to windward — Off the wind — Kicking straps again —
Holding the tiller extension and mainsheet—Changing tack—
Spilling wind—Considerations of planing—Playing the mainsail
—Meeting wind shifts—Preventing a capsize to windward—
Steering to windward—Tiller waggling—Feeling the helm—
Producing balance—Planing and running in heavy weather .. 86

X HELMING (3) — POSITIONS AND PREDICAMENTS.
Sitting out—Positions when beating or running—Getting off the
mud—Bent centreplate—What to expect from your dinghy—
Sailing limitations—Safety of others—Assisting a capsized
dinghy's crew   ..   ..
97

XI MAINTENANCE OF THE HULL. Specialized nature of
maintenance—When and where to work—Interior—Centreboard
slot rubber—Removing the oil film—Rubbing down—The art of
varnishing—Dangers of short cuts—Deep scratches—Preparing
to varnish—Varnishing   101

XII MAINTENANCE OF SPARS, RIGGING, SAILS AND
GEAR. Better sure than sorry—Stretch in new wire—Masts—
Booms — Racing flags — Sheets — Toestraps — Kicking straps
—Rudders, centreboards and centreplates—Shackles, blocks,
winches and sliding goosenecks—Rudder hangings—Keel bands
—Sails—Battens—Tillers—Anchor cables   107

Appendix

I JOINING A CLUB. The objects of a sailing club—Advantages
of membership—Royal Yachting Association—Applying for club
membership—Getting a crewing job—Dinghy sailing clubs—
Advantages of the numerically large classes—Open races—Subscriptions and expenses—Sailing journals 112

II SAFETY MEASURES. Buoyancy Apparatus—Testing Buoyancy—Stopping a capsized boat drifting—Life-jackets—Righting
the boat—Getting aboard—Bailing out—Assisting others   .. 116

III SOME OF THE MANY CLUBS GIVING REGULAR
RACES FOR DINGHIES   120

INDEX   122

RACING DINGHY
HANDLING

CHAPTER I

DINGHY CLASSES

*National 12-footers — International 14-footers — 12-foot Fireflies —
National Merlin-Rockets—Hornets—10-foot 6-inch Cadets—National
Swordfish 15-footers—National 18-footers—National Redwings—14-foot
G.P.—Graduate—Fleetwind—15-foot 6-inch Kestrel—Local Classes—
New Classes*

A N ever increasing assortment of sailing dinghy classes now satisfies
a very wide range of requirements. Such great variety may even
sometimes be bewildering to the inexperienced, but the right
choice is not really difficult if approached in the proper way, as outlined
in Chapter II. Having once decided where you expect mostly to sail
and what sort of sailing attracts you most, the choice is narrowed
greatly—and simplified still more if you have decided how much to
spend.

It is impractical in this book to discuss all the different classes of
racing dinghy, but the principal ones are briefly described. The boats
specifically mentioned have gained particular popularity or prestige and
are proved suitable for the purposes for which they were designed.
They are commended as thoroughbreds giving excellent racing and
well suited to a wide variety of conditions. In addition to those mentioned, there are a number of other widespread but less known classes,
some of which are still too young to have attained the recognition they
deserve. There is also a host of local classes, built to rules or specific
designs with the object of producing boats particularly suited to the
needs and conditions of certain areas. Many of these local classes are
excellent and there are circumstances in which a special class is desirable, because it is always easier for a designer to produce a boat suitable
for known prevailing conditions, rather than one which has to be a
compromise satisfying more varied conditions. Nevertheless, it is often

doubtful if these local classes are really much better on their own stretch of water than one of the more widespread classes shortly to be mentioned, and because they are not so widespread they can seldom give such sport and competition to the really keen racing helmsman.

It should be stressed that the advantages of owning a boat sailed on a national scale are very great and it is desirable that, wherever possible, these classes be encouraged and, consequently, the sport in them increased, so that the winner of a class championship has the satisfaction of knowing that he and his boat are the best of a large number from all over the country, and not just the best in the local river. However, if everyone were to join one of the established classes there would never be any new ones introduced, which would be bad for the sport, so one should not be too dogmatic on this point.

Without experience, it is far from easy to judge a new class, either by looking at the boat itself or even sailing it; it is still more difficult after being sailed in it by a comparative expert and there are really very few dinghy sailors who can assess a boat from a set of drawings—though plenty reckon to be able to. The publicity and advertising with which some new classes are launched tends to confuse the beginner still more, for each new boat is heralded as the paragon of all boatly virtues. If any would-be racing dinghy owners are doubtful if the boats they want are in the classes briefly mentioned in this chapter, or want further advice on the choice of the right boat, I will try to help them. This is not really an invitation to a vast correspondence, but queries on this subject sent to me with 6/- to cover the cost of a reply will be answered to the best of my ability, and may avoid subsequent disappointment. Queries should state where the boat is to be based, the age and experience of the owner, the approximate funds available, what the boat is to be used for—solely for racing, or for family sailing and pottering about as well—whether she will have to lie at moorings or can be hauled out between sailing, and if it is intended to use a car and trailer to take the boat to races or places away from home. The approximate weight of helmsman and crew is also a help. If the hull is to be stored at home at any time, the size of available garage or space should be known. If it is possible to give a few details of the local sailing conditions, so much the better.

The largest racing dinghy classes numerically are the *National 12-footers*, *International 14-footers*, *National 14-foot Merlin-Rockets*, *12-foot National Fireflies*, *10-foot 6-inch Cadets*, *16-foot Hornets*, *15-foot National Swordfish* and the *National 18-footers*. These are all designed with the emphasis definitely on racing, though obviously they need not be used exclusively for racing. With the exception of the *National 18-footer*, these boats will not lie satisfactorily at moorings, unless particularly sheltered, and they should be kept out of the water when not in use; it is essential in any case, if they are to remain in first class racing condition. They are light enough for their removal from the water and their relaunching to be a fairly simple matter and in most places it is not difficult to fulfil this requirement.

Other popular classes, in which flat-out racing characteristics are modified by greater consideration for use as family boats and for inshore, estuary and inland cruising, are the *National 14-foot Redwings,* the *General Purpose 14-footers,* the *12-foot 6-inch Graduate* and the *12-foot Fleetwind.* Of these, the *Redwings* and the *G.P. 14's* can lie on reasonably sheltered moorings and could be left afloat as a rule and the last three classes are very sympathetic to the family exchequer.

It will be noted that most of the classes mentioned are either National or International. This indicates that they are under the jurisdiction of the British Royal Yachting Association (R.Y.A.), which controls the sport in this country, or under the International Yacht Racing Union (I.Y.R.U.), which has overall control of yacht racing throughout the world. Though this official recognition is often also a recommendation —and all the classes mentioned come in this category—it is not necessarily so and there have been some official failures. Conversely, the fact that a class has not official national or international status is not necessarily a reflection on its efficiency; there are plenty of such classes proving more popular, both here and abroad, than many of those officially recognized.

Some of these classes are "restricted" and some "one-design." A restricted class is governed by rules limiting certain dimensions, weights and other features, but allowing variation of design within those limits Thus, in the *National 12's* for instance, the maximum length is 12 feet, minimum beam 4 feet 6 inches, maximum sail area 90 square feet, minimum weight 190 lb. and the hulls must be clinker built, with one plank overlapping the next, but the shape of the hulls may vary a lot—also the sail plan. Many people get interest and pleasure from the comparative individuality of restricted class boats and are able to carry out their own ideas on fittings and gadgets—some even design their own boats, but this is usually left to experienced designers. There is also the added attraction that restricted class boats can often to some extent be designed to be particularly suitable for local conditions, so that an owner can, if he wants, have a boat belonging to a widespread class but having some of the advantages of a local class.

On the other hand, a one-design dinghy is more tightly constricted by rules which ensure that each boat is exactly the same as the next. This makes matters simpler because there is no choice of design, and one-design racing, being a test of sailing ability only, certainly is attractive to those who perhaps have not the time nor the desire to tune an individual restricted class dinghy; but it reduces interest in the boats from the point of view of design development and provides no scope to those inclined to experiment with new rigs and hull shapes and who take pleasure in trying to work out new ways of improving their own boats or the dinghy classes in general.

Let us now take the most important and flourishing classes one by one and sum up, as far as possible, their characteristics and main features. In most cases the cost of these boats is mentioned, but this often varies slightly according to builder—it is given only as a guide.

NATIONAL 12-FOOT

The *National 12-foot* class was introduced by the R.Y.A. in 1936 with the object of bringing the racing of thoroughbred dinghies within the means of youngsters and others unable to afford nearly £200 on the luxury of an *International 14-footer*. With a pre-war price limit of £50 without sails, the class was an immediate success and it grows by about a hundred new boats every year—by 1954 there were over 1,300 of them. The present price limit new—one of the most important class rules—is £137 10s. (1954) and, with the modern high standard of finish and equipment, this ensures exceedingly good value. These dinghies are obtainable from various builders in partly built kit form, either as the bare hull shell, or as hulls finished apart from decking, trimmings and fittings, with all the parts required for completing the job supplied; these kits are easy to complete and greatly reduce the cost.

The class has greatly exceeded its original object of merely catering for those who could afford nothing more expensive and there are many helmsmen who stick to it because they find none they like as well; many who own more expensive boats in other classes also have *National 12's* because of the splendid sport and keen competition. It is probably fair to say that this is the most successful of the racing dinghy classes in this country and it has done more than any other for the cause of dinghy sailing, for many past and present helmsmen and crews in the *National 12's* compete with success in the other small boat classes and several have represented Britain in Olympic Games sailing.

Most of the earlier *National 12's* were built to a design by Uffa Fox made available to all builders by the *"Yachting World."* These boats, known as *Uffa-Kings*, were the basis on which the class developed for many years. Although, happily, the older boats can still win races in certain conditions, there has been vigorous development in these dinghies in the past five years and several different designers are prominent in the class. It is no exaggeration that many owners get almost as much fun experimenting with new ideas as they derive from actual sailing and since these experiments are relatively cheap, many ideas can be tried which would be too expensive a gamble to chance on a larger craft—dinghies therefore keep in the forefront of development.

Partly because of lively interest in the boats themselves, partly because the class affairs are efficiently managed by committee of owners, but mainly because there is a background of exceedingly keen and friendly competition, the *National* 12's have never been more flourishing than now.

They are fast and lively on all points of sailing, especially to windward in light airs, and the modern ones in particular plane well reaching in a blow. On restricted inland waters, where there is much short tacking, they are exceptionally satisfying, owing to their responsiveness. Their small sail area of 90 square feet, with limitations on height of sail plan, makes them easily crewed by girls or youngsters—agility being of more value than brute force. Spinnakers are not allowed and this, perhaps, renders the craft more valuable and instructive as a racing class, for tactics of pure sailing are more important off the wind than the mere cramming on of extra sail. They very seldom have to reef and stand up surprisingly well to conditions of heavy weather and rough water. Decking, within limits, is optional, but most modern boats have the utmost permitted, and almost all at least have foredecks; rules insist on adequate buoyancy apparatus to keep the boat floating when filled with water and with crew aboard, and many have more than this, enabling them to be sailed after a fashion even when completely waterlogged.

A new form of construction, introduced in 1953, uses plywood planking bonded together with waterproof adhesives, and no ribs, giving a neater internal structure. This construction has so far proved very satisfactory, and almost all new boats are built this way, but of course there is not yet long enough experience to prove that it will stand the test of time—though it certainly promises to do so.

The second-hand price for a good boat in 1955 is about £120, though they can be had for only £40, whilst very successful dinghies command a premium at about £140. Bare hulls can be had from the best builders for as little as £47.

INTERNATIONAL 14-FOOT
It is upon foundations laid by this class in the past that the sport of dinghy racing, as we know it now, has developed and prospered. The *International* 14's achieved international status in 1927 and are sailed in U.S.A., Canada, Bermuda and New Zealand, as well as in this country, but though an older class than the *National* 12's, they are not as numerous in Britain, probably mainly on account of their cost. As aristocrats of the dinghy world, they have always been expensive for their size and there has never been any price limitation. Like the *National* 12's, it is a restricted class, in which considerable variation in design is permitted.

Prior to 1949 most of the up-to-date 14's were carvel built, with smooth skins, there usually being two layers of mahogany planking secured to light ribs by nailing. By 1949 the cost of such dinghies had risen to about £400, and expense was keeping young helmsmen out of the class. That year an effort was made to reduce the cost of new boats; a clinker planked boat was first built and was quite successful, but soon afterwards Fairey Marine Company introduced a moulded carvel hull designed by Uffa Fox, who had designed the great majority of the most successful dinghies in the previous two decades.

The moulded boats are built of several layers of thin veneer bonded together under pressure and heat with a synthetic resin glue, giving a smooth skin both inside and out. Since these hot moulded boats have been on the market, the majority have been of this type, though there have been some notably successful exceptions which have been individually built by hand moulding methods producing similar results without the need for expensive moulds. The mass production of the *International* 14's has brought the price down to about £350 for a complete boat, but inevitably individuality has had to be sacrificed to economy, possibly with some consequent slowing of development. The clinker built 14's cost about £230. Hand-moulded boats can cost from £250-£700, according to builder, and hulls in partly finished form as little as £83. The cheaper hand-moulded 14's and partly finished boats only came on the market late in 1954 and may do much to revive interest in the class.

Decking is prohibited by the class rules and the class prides itself on being one of the few entirely open racing dinghies remaining. In 1954, however, it passed rules allowing automatic self-bailers which drain spray out of the boat and will even dry it out very quickly after swamping or capsizing. At the same time the buoyancy rules were revised so that more adequate buoyancy could be provided.

Carrying a relatively large sail area—and spinnakers which may, in fact, double the measured sail area off the wind—they are fairly hard work to sail and need a tough crew in a blow, though most modern hulls are more stable and powerful than those of a few years ago. Taken all round, they are faster than most other racing dinghies of their length.

In spite of worthy efforts to reduce the cost of these boats, which have to a great extent succeeded, they will still remain more expensive than the *Merlin-Rockets* and 12-foot dinghy classes. There may be almost as much fun—perhaps quite as much fun—racing in the cheaper classes but the *International* 14's have great aesthetic value. It is hoped, and anticipated, that those who can afford to race them will continue to do so.

12-FOOT NATIONAL FIREFLIES

This strictly one-design boat was introduced by the R.Y.A. in 1946 in an effort to combat the effects of post-war rising costs and to try to provide a good type of racing boat that would still be within the means of the young and less affluent. Unfortunately the original target price of about £65 rose until by 1951 it was almost identical with that of the *National* 12's for boats equipped with the same essential racing gear. However, the ease of maintenance and one-design simplicity of these boats does mean low upkeep costs.

Methods of construction developed in the war in the aircraft industry are used in *Fireflies*, which are built exclusively by Fairey Marine Company to an Uffa Fox design. The smooth skin is multiplywood moulded under considerable pressure and heat; it is light, strong and the interior smoothness makes them easy to keep clean and in good condition. The hull is 30 lb. lighter than that of a *National* 12, though the centreplate and the aluminium mast and boom are heavier than those usually in modern *Nationals*.

Under most conditions the *Fireflies* have about the same performance as the *National* 12's. They are slower than good *National* 12's in light and medium winds, but in strong winds may be a little faster to windward, though they do not plane so readily. Their rather fuller sections make them a little more stable and easier to sail.

They are good seaboats, though wetter than the *National* 12's, and have a foredeck and side decks. The standard buoyancy apparatus gives less support to a capsized boat than does that in modern *National* 12's.

The strict one-designedness of this class attracts those who perhaps have not the time, desire or knowledge to tune the individual type of restricted class dinghy (though this is usually unnecessary if the boat comes from a reputable builder and designer). *Fireflies* are commonly adopted as club-owned boats for this reason, as they stand a lot of ill treatment without suffering unduly—nearly eight per cent. of them are communally owned.

NATIONAL MERLIN-ROCKET 14-FOOTER

This is the most recent of the dinghy classes to come under R.Y.A. jurisdiction and assume national status, and is really a combination of two classes—the *Merlins* and the *Rockets*—to form a single united one with modified rules fitting them both. The merging took place in 1951 and since that time the united class has grown vigorously, until it is now Britain's second largest restricted class. The majority of the new boats have a character midway between their original antecedents, but because the two basically different original types are both within the framework of the rules, the class is extremely versatile and includes boats suitable for almost any conditions practical for racing dinghies. The appeal of the *Merlin-Rocket* is therefore widespread and it has a great future before it, especially as a rule restricts the maximum price of both new and second-hand boats to £160 without sails (1954).

The original *Merlin* class was introduced in 1946 when the "*Yachting World*" published sets of plans from a design by Jack Holt and a set of rules. During the early days of the class, most *Merlins* had very tall rigs, but in the two years before the merger the majority of new boats were flatter in the hull and had a lower sail plan, making them more stable. These *Merlins* were completely decked in except for a short narrow cockpit. About two hundred and forty had been built up to the time of the merger.

The *Rockets* were introduced in 1950 to provide a boat more docile than other thoroughbred racing dinghies then existing, yet retaining the lively "feel" and other attractive qualities of the modern planing types. They were, in fact, intended to be suitable for family racing and sailing; the rules permitted three to be carried as crew, so that children could sometimes be taken racing with their parents and learn from them the management of a boat (this is no longer allowed under the rules of the merged *Merlin-Rockets*). Although the *Rockets* were allowed to be entirely undecked, the majority had foredecks and fairly narrow sidedecks. The freeboard was greater than the *Merlins* and the sail plan lower. On the whole, in light airs they were slower than *Merlins*, but as fast in a blow. A design, by Digby Coppock, to which most of the boats in the class were built, was published by "*The Yachtsman*" and about eighty boats were built or building when the merger took place.

The *Merlin-Rockets*—like the *National 12's*—have to be clinker-built and most of the new boats, of which the majority are hybrids between the two original types, have planking of special plywood bonded together with synthetic adhesives; there are no ribs and the interior is neater and easier to keep in good condition. They can be bought as partially built kits, which much reduces the cost.

Though, like every other racing dinghy, their sensitivity demands much of the helmsman and crew for them to sail at their best, they are a little easier to manage than *National 12's* and *Fireflies*. They are less work to sail than *International 14's* because of their smaller sail area. Most of them plane very easily and fast and are dry and seaworthy. They carry very adequate buoyancy apparatus—sufficient to float a completely waterlogged boat with the crew both aboard. There is a price rule restricting the cost to £160 new, without sails (1954). Second-hand boats sell for about £140 complete; prefabricated kits of parts are available and bare hulls cost £62 10s.

A 14-foot *National Merlin-Rocket* planing.   The boat is upright even in this weight of wind and the helmsman and crew lean out together, with the helmsman looking over the top of the crew, presenting as little windage as possible.

The prototype of the *Cadet* class sailing at Putney. This boat is designed to be suitable for youngsters and the sail area is not too much for children to manage

16-FOOT HORNET

Until the end of 1951, when the *Hornet* was introduced by the "*Yachting World,*" there was a gap between the light, fast planing 14-footers and the heavy almost non-planing *National* 18's. The *Hornet*, designed by Jack Holt, being of light modern construction, yet longer than the 14-footers, quickly demonstrated the potential speeds that longer light displacement hulls might be expected to achieve.

The crew of a *Hornet* sits on a plank which can be slid out to windward; the crew's feet normally rest on the gunwale and when he is sitting right on the end of the plank, the power of the boat to carry sail is greatly increased. The sail area is small for the size of boat and the ease with which the jib can be managed and the help given by the sliding seat make them popular with girl crews, though heavy crews are certainly an advantage when it blows hard. In spite of the small sail area, to which is added a spinnaker, *Hornets* are lively under all conditions, though slower than the *Merlin-Rockets* in light airs. They plane very easily and are most exciting in a good breeze. Most of them have self-draining cockpits, so that capsizing is only a matter of having to right the boat again and sailing on.

Three hundred *Hornets* were built in the first three years of the class, their popularity being partly due to the low cost and simplicity of building the hard-chine hull from kits of parts. Hull shape and sail plan are one-design, but there is some scope for individuality in the layout of the decking. They cost about £180 without sails and complete kits of prefabricated parts and fittings are about £83, excluding sails.

10-FOOT 6-INCH CADET

To encourage young people to sail and own their own boats, the "*Yachting World*" commissioned Jack Holt to design the *Cadet* in 1947. One of the most important rules of the class is that, to take part in official races, the helmsman must not be more than eighteen years old. The class is thus assured of remaining a junior one and it is a great success. The *Cadets* are numerically the largest racing class in Britain.

The design has proved itself well suited to the requirements, the pram bow contributing to good balance and easy handling and preventing the nasty habit in some short boats of trying to nosedive when running before a strong wind.

The class holds championship races in just the same way as the other dinghy classes and the top standard of helmsmanship is high. Though intended for youngsters, it should not be supposed that the *Cadets* are completely foolproof, for they are meant for boys and girls who are prepared to learn to sail properly. The absolutely safe centre-board boat does not exist; if it did, it would probably be tediously clumsy, slow and uninteresting. In sailing boats, like most other things, you cannot eat your cake and have it too—either you have a fast and lively boat requiring proper handling, or else a slow old tub that bores you to tears. The *Cadet* is a little thoroughbred and deserves to be treated as such.

The hull is hard-chine construction, with plywood skin. The small sail area is well within the strength of young people to manage; the jib need not be used by beginners or when cruising, but the perform-ance is much improved by it, in spite of its tiny area. There is also a small spinnaker, which gives valuable training and maintains the crew's sense of responsibility and interest when running. The hull is well decked in and will float on its side when capsized without taking water into the cockpit; inflated rubber buoyancy bags fore and aft provide very adequate buoyancy apparatus. *Cadets* will lie safely on sheltered moorings. Plans for building them are obtainable from the "*Yachting World*" and the majority of *Cadets* have been built at home from sets of prefabricated parts, which cost £45, without sails. Com-plete boats, with sails, cost about £81.

SWORDFISH NATIONAL 15-FOOTER

The 15-*foot Swordfish* was introduced by the R.Y.A. as a national one-design class in 1946. Designed by Uffa Fox it is built by Fairey Marine in the same construction as the *Firefly*. Though this class has much to commend it, it has never achieved the popularity of the *National 12's*, *Fireflies* and *Merlin-Rockets*.

From the family-man's point of view, one of the attractive features not shared by any other National dinghy class is that a crew of three is permitted. This makes the *Swordfish* valuable for training novices in the art of crewing and helming. With three to sail the boat, the two experienced hands can do most of the work during a race, relieving the novice of most of the responsibility which might tend to fluster or worry and depress him if he were expected to take a full half-share right away. In the earlier stages of learning to race, perhaps more knowledge is gained by watching than by doing.

Swordfish, owing to the weight of their centreplate and their com-paratively great wetted surface, are not so fast as modern *Merlin-Rockets*, but their initial stability is considerably greater. They have both foredeck and side-decks, but are roomy and comfortable providing you keep your head out of the way of the low boom which is only fifteen inches above the deck. Their moderate sail area is easy to manage; the foresail is only 4 square feet bigger than a *National 12's*; but the spinnaker is considerably bigger than a *Merlin-Rocket's*. The boats are rather cumbersome to handle out of the water because of their heavy centreplates, but they ride reasonably well on moorings in sheltered positions if necessary. They cost £215, without sails.

NATIONAL 18-FOOTER

The *National* 18's, by virtue of their weight and robustness rather than size, really come between the dinghy classes and the small keel boat classes. The minimum weight allowed for the centreplate alone is only 15 lb. less than the weight of a complete *National* 12 hull and though trailing a *National* 18 is quite practical, it is a major operation compared with the lighter boats.

It is a restricted class, the rules being similar in many ways to a scaled up version of the *National* 12's, the boats being similar in many ways. The 18's carry spinnakers and 190 square feet of working sail—more than twice that of the 12's—but they are stable enough to carry it well. Speed to windward is good, but their performance off the wind suffers because of their weight, though they will plane sometimes. They usually lie on moorings and are excellent and safe seaboats.

14-FOOT NATIONAL REDWINGS

These clinker-built one-design dinghies were designed for the Looe Sailing Club just before the war by Uffa Fox. They became popular throughout Devon and Cornwall and in 1954 applied for and were granted national status, with 183 boats in the class. They are tough, stable, and can lie on moorings. Their heaviness is detrimental to their performance, particularly planing, but they are very seaworthy and stand up well to rough conditions.

14-FOOT GENERAL PURPOSE DINGHY

Although it was never intended as a racing class, the "*Yachting World*" General Purpose 14's are raced considerably and hold annual championships. They are powerful and fairly beamy hard-chine 14-footers with good stability and handling qualities and though they have not a comparable performance with the out-and-out racing 14-footers, they nevertheless have a fair turn of speed and give good sport. They are cheap and simple to build from kits of prefabricated parts, and are light and easily trailed. In fact, this is an economical and thoroughly healthy type of beginner's boat. The cost, complete with sails, is about £135, but complete kits of prefabricated parts cost £97.

12-FOOT 6-INCH GRADUATE

The *Graduate*, designed and built by Wyche & Coppock, who produce many of Britain's best known *Merlin-Rockets* and *National* 12's, was introduced by *"Light Craft"* in 1952 as a cheap racing and cruising dinghy. Although not so fast as a *National* 12, its lightness greatly helps its performance, which does not fall far short of that of the more specialized racing dinghy, and its stability is greater.

The boat has been specially designed for cheap building and amateur construction from scratch or from kits of parts. It is hard-chine and greatly strengthened by bulkheads at each end of the cockpit, forming watertight compartments fore and aft for buoyancy when waterlogged and the dry stowage of light gear. More than 180 boats were built in the first two years of this class. Complete with sails they cost only £95, and complete kits of parts for building, including sails, £73.

FLEETWIND 12-FOOTER

An inexpensive hard-chine utility racing dinghy which gives good sport for its cost, and as a result is gaining in popularity.

15-FOOT 6-INCH KESTREL

The *Kestrel* was designed by me in 1953 in answer to the plea for a true family racing boat—something which would be really satisfying to race hard sometimes, but which would be safe and particularly easy to handle when not racing. The *Kestrel* also had to have a good performance with only two aboard, yet also sail well with three adults or two adults and two children and for this reason a round bilged type was chosen. A versatile boat resulted with a performance similar to the *Merlin-Rockets*, but considerably easier to sail, the handling qualities in strong winds and planing giving great confidence.

The clinker-built hull is strong enough to come to no harm if the boat has to take the ground on a mooring which dries out at low tide, but is light enough to be trailed easily or taken ashore between sailing. They have ridden out really nasty conditions on exposed moorings.

The sail plan is fairly low, to aid stability, but the boom is well lifted for the sake of comfort and good visibility. For racing or light winds there is a good sized jib, while for cruising or racing with a child crew there is a smaller jib; there is also a moderate sized spinnaker. As three can race as crew in this class, there are the same advantages for training youngsters as were mentioned in the note on *Swordfish*.

They cost about £180, without sails, or £83, as kits. Fibreglass is being investigated as an alternative construction.

NEW CLASSES

Most prominent in the public eye as this edition is being prepared is the *Five-O-Five* class, which was introduced in 1954 by *"Yachts and Yachting."* This high performance 16-foot 6-inch moulded plywood boat is a slightly smaller and modified version of John Westell's *Coronet* which came third to my own 17-foot 6-inch *Osprey* in the Coronation Round the Island dinghy race and subsequently did very well in the 1953 International Two-man trials. A notable feature of the design is the wide concave flare in the topsides, which increases the beam at deck level—and hence the sitting out power of the crew—without increasing the beam at water level; this helps to keep the spray out of the boat. Every effort has been made to reduce the weight as much as possible and with her greater length and the same sail area, a *Five-O-Five* is faster than an *International* 14 in moderate and fresh winds. They will not lie happily on moorings. They require considerable weight and strength to hold them up in a breeze of wind and they are £40 more expensive than even the *International* 14's, but the class has been sponsored with much energy and enthusiasm and is likely to become firmly established.

Another new class is the 18-*foot Jollyboat* designed by Uffa Fox and built by Fairey Marine. This is a faster planer than the *Five-O-Five*, but slightly slower in light airs on the whole. She is designed to sail with three aboard most of the time and her sedateness in changing from one tack to the other makes her suitable for less agile dinghy sailors. Though larger than the *Five-O-Five*, she costs the same.

There are signs of other new classes on the way, but it is too early to say much about them.

LOCAL CLASSES

There is now such a wide selection of official or unofficial national classes from which to choose that one or other of them is almost bound to suit almost any local conditions. The tendency is for local classes to be gradually replaced by more modern and widespread classes, but circumstances certainly do exist in some places where a specially designed boat is desirable. One of the principal drawbacks to local classes is that the secondhand market is obviously restricted and now that trailing dinghies around from one race to another in various parts of the country has become so popular, classes which are sailed only locally miss some of the fun.

OTHER CLASSES

As was said at the beginning of this chapter, it is impossible to mention every good dinghy class in a book of this nature. There are many other excellent, if less known classes and I can only apologise to their supporters for having had to omit them.

CHAPTER II

BUYING A BOAT

Choice of class—Cost—Moorings or stowage ashore—Portability—What will you use her for?—Local sailing conditions—Choosing the design or build—Finding a second-hand boat—Racing records—Condition—Defects

IN choosing the boat you are to own there are a number of factors to be considered. If you are fairly new to the sailing game it would, possibly, not be wise to put a great deal of money into one of the more expensive types. Once people start to race dinghies they usually find it very hard to get enough of it. There are, of course, exceptional folk who come to the conclusion that there are more desirable ways of spending their free time than being doubled up in a small boat trying to squeeze her along in hardly any wind, or relying on the goodwill of their tummy muscles and the purchase of their toes under a canvas strap to suspend them over the gunwale, where every other wave comes up and slaps their posterior anatomy. Lest you be scared away at this point, let me hasten to add that there are many who become so keen on this kind of treatment that they frequently travel fifty miles and more on winter week-ends, to race under conditions in which bilge water sometimes forms an icy slush in the bottom of the boat and spray freezes the sails hard and stiff. Believe it or not, dinghyites have actually been seen to laugh as though they were really enjoying it when swimming alongside their dinghy capsized in a January gale! It will be admitted that there must undoubtedly be some strange fascination in the sport to permit such a phenomenon.

A great deal of help in choosing the right kind of boat is generally forthcoming from the local club (see Appendix I), whose members will know the conditions with which your dinghy will have to contend. As a rule, sailing folk are very willing to give help and advice. Try to get your information from a dinghy specialist—someone who sails them himself; there are many who sail in other types of boat who are not fully conversant with the modern type of racing dinghy.

One of the most important factors which will govern your choice is the amount of money you are prepared to spend on your dinghy. The cheapest one is the *Cadet*, but this will be no use to you as a racing boat if you are older than eighteen. Next follows the *Firefly*, with the *National* 12 in very close company; costing about a third as much again is the *Merlin-Rocket*, followed next by the *Swordfish*; then comes the *International* 14-*footer*, and most expensive of all is the *National* 18-*footer*, at more than twice the cost of a *National* 12. As a very rough guide to help you budget for your expenditure, you may take it that it will cost you about £5 a year on materials to keep your dinghy in proper trim, if you do the work yourself; in addition to this, there will be your subscription to the club, race entry fees and, possibly, cost of storage—these items are dealt with in Appendix I. If you have not the time or inclination to do your own maintenance work, this may cost you quite a bit. New sails, required about every five years, cost anything from £15 to £50 according to area and finish. A suit for a *National* 12 costs about £22 (1954). There will also be certain extras to be acquired when you purchase the boat, though when buying second-hand you will probably get these included in the sale of the dinghy herself—they are mentioned a little later in this chapter. If you are most unfortunate or careless, your mast might break and that may cost you anything from £3 to £35 to replace, according to the type of boat. Premiums for the insurance of racing dinghies are generally rather high, but when racing in big fleets it is generally advisable to insure.

The next most important question to be considered is, where is your boat to be kept when you are not sailing her? If she has to lie on exposed moorings, then none of the classes specifically mentioned are really suitable, except the *National* 18-*footer* and the 15 foot 6 inch *Kestrel*. On sheltered waters, the *Swordfish, Cadet* and *Firefly* could be moored out reasonably safely and, if the mooring was exceptionally sheltered, any of the dinghies mentioned could be left afloat, even though this would be most undesirable. If she is to be any use as a racing boat, a dinghy of the *International* 14, the *National* 12, or the *Merlin-Rocket* class must be kept out of the water when she is not being sailed, in order to prevent the hull from becoming saturated with moisture and the surface of the bottom from deteriorating. Boats with plywood skins, such as the *Cadet, Firefly* and *Swordfish*, are not so badly affected, but should, if possible, be kept ashore too. Remember that others will also probably want to get their dinghies ashore after racing, and so there will be many willing hands to help you if assistance is given in return, when others want a lift. So, if somewhere to keep your boat is not immediately obvious near to the club, as it will be in many cases, have a look around for suitable places nearby. Dinghies can be, and frequently are, launched from a beach, and it is the practice at some dinghy racing centres to remove the masts from the boats when they are ashore and wheel the hulls away from the water and into sheds on trolleys. This is very little trouble and is certainly best for the dinghies.

Another thing to be considered is whether you will wish to take your boat away when you go for a holiday, or if you want to compete in open races on other stretches of water than those which you have chosen as your home area. A great number—in fact the majority—of racing dinghies in the classes mentioned sail in open races once or twice a year at least, and are taken on a trailer, behind a car, to these races. The lighter the boat, the easier it is to do this; the *National* 18 *footer* is a little too big for easy handling, and the *Swordfish* just about as large as one would generally wish to tackle. The others are easy.

You should also think of the uses to which your dinghy will be put. Do you want merely to race, or do you want to be able to take the family out for a picnic as well? All of these dinghies are excellent for cruising and can, of course, be sailed under reduced rig, but there is not much room for picnicking in *Cadets*, *Fireflies*, *National* 12's or *Merlin-Rockets*, nor is it a good thing to put an *International* 14 to such use. The *Kestrel*, *Swordfish* and the *National* 18 are suitable for this kind of thing and make good family boats. Do not suppose that it is impossible to take a third person afloat in a *National* 12 or a *Firefly* especially when the addition is not too hefty, but it is not very good for the boat and comfort will be at about the standard achieved in the Eton Wall Game and one's picnic tea not unlike the scramble for the largest piece of pancake on Shrove Tuesday at Westminster.

As far as suitability to racing conditions is concerned, there is not a lot to choose between them, for all are excellent sea boats, though because of her size, there are limitations in the case of the *Cadet*, which, though very able, should not be subjected to a very short sea. The *Fireflies*, *National* 12's, *International* 14's and *Merlin-Rockets* will stand up to a great deal, but perhaps a generously decked-in *Kestrel*, the *Swordfish*, and heavier *Redwing* will take more punishment; the *National* 18 is the toughest of them all. Unless you know the locality really well, do not judge the water on which you are to race by casual observation; it is deceptive and what may appear to be a peaceful land-locked stretch of friendly and inviting wetness at the time you look at it, may have strong currents, shallows and wind funnels, which whip the surface into a most jagged-looking mass of broken water when conditions are bad.

Having decided on the class of boat you want, you will now have to set about getting her. In the club you have joined you will probably find yachting periodicals and publications in which dinghy races are reported, and from these reports—if they are good ones—you should be able to learn the names of the builders or designers of some of the best boats. If you have a look around at a few racing dinghies and follow the results of some of the bigger races, you should soon be able to pick out the reliable builders. Builders' name-plates usually appear somewhere on the dinghy, generally on the centre thwart or the inside of the transom. Furthermore, there may be a good local boatbuilder who is to be recommended, but he should be one who specializes in, or has particular knowledge of, racing dinghies, because many of the best builders of larger craft make quite a poor job of a racing dinghy. If you are having a new boat built to a fresh design, you should definitely have an agreement with the builder to the effect that the dinghy will not be accepted by you unless she is able to pass the class rules when measured and weighed; she would otherwise be useless to you. The price paid will, of course, have to be within the limit laid down in the class rules, if there is any such restriction; the rules should be obtained from the Secretary of the R.Y.A. or the class Secretary, so that a check may be kept on these things. It is common practice for a deposit of one-third of the agreed final cost of the boat to be paid when work commences on her, another third when the hull is planked and the remainder on delivery. *Fireflies* and *Swordfish* are mass-produced at the present time and are only obtainable from one builder.

Second-hand racing dinghies are advertised for sale in the yachting press and from a perusal of several back numbers it should be possible to judge the current prices. The club Secretary may also know of a second-hand boat to be bought in the district and, quite frequently, notices advertising boats for sale are posted on club notice boards. As a rule it is cheaper to buy a boat in the autumn, but this is not so in the case of racing dinghies, the value of which does not fluctuate with the time of year to any great extent.

As with racehorses, the most important thing to be considered when purchasing a dinghy for racing is her racing record, and you should take pains to find out, when buying a second-hand boat, how she has been performing recently. In restricted classes there is, of course, owing to progress in the class, a tendency for the newer boats to be a little faster, but there are many old boats that are able to give a good account of themselves amongst much younger rivals, especially in the *National* 12-*foot* class; for, although hull shape cannot be altered from the original as a general rule (though it has, to a limited extent, been done in certain cases), it is often possible, in these restricted classes, to incorporate improvements in rig and so on by a few simple modifications as they become of proven value. As *Merlin-Rockets* are a developing class, the age of the boat should be considered, but, naturally, in the one-design classes such as the *Fireflies* and *Swordfish* the age is quite immaterial so long as the hull is in a good state.

The condition of most racing dinghies, even those of a considerable age, is usually of a high standard, because most of them are treated very carefully and kept dry when not in use. The most common and important defects to be found are broken ribs and cracked garboard

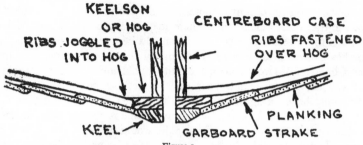

Figure 2

strakes—these are the planks nearest the keel. The garboards in some *National* 12's were very wide and susceptible to splitting. In any case the garboards should be inspected and also the inside of the centreboard case and the centreboard slot in the keel, where the wood is liable to suffer most deterioration as it cannot be very well protected by paint or varnish. The ribs, where they are fastened to the keelson (the inner part of the keel), may also show signs of weakening. Figure 2, which shows two alternative methods of fastening the ribs, will give an indication of the position of the parts mentioned. A dinghy should not be condemned outright because of broken ribs or even a cracked garboard or other plank, for these can be made good by a skilful boatbuilder, but, of course, this costs money and an allowance should be made for it in the price paid. Soft and mushy keels, keelsons, centreboard cases and garboards are a more serious matter.

The manner in which a dinghy has been stored will have much to do with her value, so be observant of the conditions under which she has been kept. If she has been carelessly slung up by ropes under a hot roof for a while, or left to lie on her side or at some other odd angle in the corner of a shed, her worth as a racing boat may be almost nil, for she may very possibly have lost her proper shape. At some clubs, dinghies are slung up on beams which support their keels and this, of course, has no detrimental effect on them, for the keel is designed to take the weight of the boat—it is when the planking is called upon to take some of the weight that the damage is done. The state of the varnish or paintwork is not of vital importance, though a dinghy with a well-kept surface is naturally a better buy than one which will require a lot of work to be expended upon her before you can make her sleek, smooth and beautiful. A few battle scars and scratches on the sides and bottom are to be expected and are not usually serious—though they may be if they are very deep—but they will generally be removed by a careful owner.

The mast should be given a close inspection. See that it is not bent or twisted, as, although it may be possible to cure this, it is often a difficult and sometimes an impossible task. The state of the rigging wire or rope is not of much importance as this should be renewed as a matter of course on buying the boat, unless it is obviously in first-class order ; but the tangs or plates, whereby the rigging is fastened to the mast, should be looked at, as it is a serious matter if these are working loose from the wood—for one cannot go on putting new fastenings into hollow masts indefinitely without the mast becoming considerably weakened. Cracks down the glued joints of hollow masts are not really serious, as they can probably be glued up again, though naturally they are undesirable. The most important defects to look out for in the sails are patches of rot or mildew reducing the strength of the canvas, and, in the case of badly affected sails, it may be possible to tear holes in them with your fingernails. Also see that the seams are strong and that the twine holding the bolt ropes (the rope round the sail edges) is not rotten or chafed through, by simply giving a moderately sharp tug, as though to pull the rope from the sail—this may evoke protest from the owner, but should not worry him if the sails are sound. The cloth around the headboard, at the upper corner or head of a mainsail, may be chafed, as may also be the inner ends of the batten pockets. The wire luff rope sewn into the leading edge of the foresail may be rusty and, if so, it may very likely have affected the cloth close to it. Bend the luff of the sail backwards and forwards close to your ear and you may be able to hear broken ends parting or rubbing against the canvas. Most of these defects can be made good by the maker of the sails (his name will usually be found at the bottom leading corner, or tack, of the sail), but, of course, there is no hope for sails whose fabric is weakened throughout by rot.

Most of the other defects which may exist will be obvious, and it should not be difficult to judge if they are easily made good or not, the value of the boat varying accordingly. The buying of a racing dinghy is not a simple matter and it is easier to be "had" when doing so than it is when purchasing most other things. The help of an experienced dinghy sailor will be invaluable.

A new dinghy will have to be measured by one of the R.Y.A., Club or Class Official Measurers, and a certificate issued giving the dimensions and certifying that the boat can legitimately race in her class. The Secretary of the R.Y.A., or of the class, will be able to give a list of Official Measurers, of which there are a number, each one dealing with a specific area. Second-hand boats should have a valid certificate, which has to be endorsed yearly to the effect that the dinghy has been tested for buoyancy when waterlogged and supporting a specified weight of iron for the required time. In the case of all classes, this certificate will have to be dated 1946 or later, as all racing dinghies had to be remeasured after the war. If no such certificate is forthcoming with the boat, you will have to have her remeasured. The fact that a dinghy has a class sail number does not necessarily mean that she has ever been measured, or even that she will be within the correct dimensions when she is measured; so beware, for she may be unable to race in the class and it would indeed be a bitter experience to buy such a boat and be banned from racing in the class you have chosen to support. Application for the class number is made to the controlling body of the class and this will usually be done by the builder as soon as, or before, work is commenced on the hull; as soon as it is obtained, see that your sails are ordered so that you will have a better chance of getting them by the time the boat is ready for you. All that was said concerning the desirability of choosing a reliable builder applies no less to the case of the sailmaker. Poor sails may even be a worse handicap than a poor boat.

The equipment that is needed for a racing dinghy is generally as follows, though of course there is some variation according to the class: hull, mast, boom, centreboard, rudder, tiller, buoyancy apparatus, floorboards, and all standing and running rigging and essential fittings are considered to be part and parcel of the boat and count towards the maximum price in such classes as have a price rule. In addition to these things you should have a mainsail, foresail, sail battens (three for *Cadets*, *National* 12's and *Fireflies*; four for *International* 14's, *Merlins*, *Swordfish* and *National* 18's), sail bag, racing flag or burgee, jib stick or spinnaker and spinnaker boom, top and bottom covers, bailer, sponge, 2½- to 5-pound kedge anchor and line, kicking strap (see Figure I), toestraps and paddle. There are numerous other extras which are used in some classes, but the list given should contain all the essentials for a fully and properly equipped racing dinghy, except for a good crew and a skipper with a hardy constitution.

CHAPTER III

CREWING (1)—RIGGING AND JOBS ASHORE

Importance of good crewing—What to wear—Rigging—Shrouds and fore-stay—Sails—Battens—The mainsheet—Hoisting sails—The kicking strap—Check of gear—Time check—Starting signals

A GOOD crew is of the utmost importance as a race-winning factor. All the efforts of the helmsman to steer his dinghy on the most advantageous course and the thought and skill put into the design, construction and maintenance of his craft, can be nullified by a careless and poor foresheet hand. Teamwork is the thing that wins races, the team being the helmsman, the crew, and the boat. No member of the team is much more important than the other.

As already mentioned, there is no better way of learning to race your own boat than by crewing for a good helmsman, but crewing should not necessarily be regarded simply as a stepping-stone towards helming and skilful ownership. A really first-class crew is worth his weight in gold and is constantly sought after by helmsmen for big and important races; therefore, someone who specializes in this task and sets out to make himself a really top-line foresheet hand, may have the great satisfaction of crewing numbers of winning dinghies and may very well consider crewing as an end in itself and a job worthy of receiving his continued attention, rather than just a rung on the ladder to good helmsmanship.

Good crewing starts ashore, before ever the dinghy is put afloat, if she is not kept on the water. Let us, then, start from the beginning.

Firstly, consider your own comfort, for there is little time during a race for ministering to it. Granted that the racing of dinghies is a far from comfortable pastime and in fact frequently causes acute physical discomfort, as indeed do most sports (consider the tramplings one gets beneath rugger scrums, the odd bump from fast bowlers, one's hands after the first hard game of fives and the effect of long rides on horseback at infrequent intervals)—still it is a mistake to ignore comfort altogether. To be warm and as comfortable as possible when afloat means that you will sail better; a wet, shivering, chafed and bruised dinghy-sailer seldom functions at his best; furthermore, the correct clothes will contribute much to your pleasure. The following will be a guide. The right footgear is, obviously, light canvas shoes with rubber soles; it may seem a somewhat sacrilegious suggestion, but a hole cut in the toe of each shoe will increase your comfort, as it will allow water to run out of them instead of being trapped so that you feel as if you had both feet in water buckets. Generally speaking, it is far colder afloat than it is ashore; this is especially true in warmer weather, but on cold, wintry, blowy days it is surprising how warm the exertion of sailing keeps one. Light windproof smocks or jackets over sweaters are the best rig above the waist, and a scarf tucked in at the neck will stop any spray going down and keep some of the draught out. Whenever possible, shorts should be worn, as they give freedom of movement, but if trousers are preferred they should be on the short side; skirts and kilts are not to be recommended. Again it should be emphasized that light windproof material is better than thicker cloth, which becomes heavy and remains damp for a long time if it gets wet. In boisterous weather a tough pair of canvas shorts worn outside another pair of shorts or trousers will mean that less demand is made upon the wearing qualities of the epidermis of the portion of anatomy which they cover. Socks or stockings usually get wet at the outset, but even so, may help to keep the feet warm in colder weather; in the sun one is better off without them, as canvas shoes quickly dry. Headgear is not usually worn in dinghies, but the glare from white sails and water may be considerable and something with a peak or eyeshield may be a comfort on bright days. Dark glasses may also be worn, but it may be found that these have the effect of making it difficult to judge distances. Goggles with deep yellow or orange lenses enable the wearer to see with great clarity and it is certainly possible to recognize marks and other objects from a far greater distance, in hazy weather, when using such lenses. Girls, poets and musicians with long hair should tie it up securely; otherwise it is liable to get caught in the kicking strap, tangled in the rigging, or blown across their own or the helmsman's face, and so to block the view at some crucial moment in a tricky manoeuvre. Spray is apt to produce permanent waves of its own design, which may not agree with the desires of the hairdresser.

Now let us get down to the job of rigging the boat. If she is stored inside a shed or without her mast, this will have to be stepped. The method of stepping will vary with different types of mast; those stepped on the keel are easier, if anything, to put in. There is a knack in handling masts, and it is very simple once this knack, which is merely a question of feeling its balance properly, is mastered. It is an operation which most owners will prefer to carry out themselves and it is, therefore, dealt with in Chapter V, in which diagrams appear to illustrate the types of steppings in most common use. The crew will probably be called upon to fasten the rigging screws, however, and, if this is done by screwing together the parts of the rigging screw itself, care should be taken to see that the threads of each end are entered into the body at the same time; this will mean unscrewing one of them a bit before entering the other (see Figure 3). In most dinghies the rigging screws are attached to the shroud plates by steel pins and the screw is not unthreaded to remove the mast—this means that the adjustment of the rake of the mast is not altered every time the mast is taken down (see Figure 4). In some instances there is no rigging screw, but just an eye spliced into the shroud. In these cases make quite certain that the split pin, safety pin or seizing wire retaining the steel pin in position, is quite secure. The shrouds and forestay of a *Cadet* are held by lanyards spliced to eyes in the end of the wire rigging. These lanyards should be wetted, after they have been set up, to shrink them and put greater tension on the shrouds. Adjustment to the mast and tension on the shrouds will generally be carried out by the skipper. If you are called upon to carry the mast, you will probably find it surprisingly light. It should, of course, be carried at the centre of gravity or point of balance, which will be about three-eighths of the way from the heel. Have a look for thin flag halliards on the mast before it goes up; if there are none there, it means that the racing flag should be fixed to the mast before it is put up and you should point out to your skipper that it is missing—it would mean rolling the boat on her side to fix it later on.

Figure 3

After the mast is up and the shrouds and forestay properly tensioned, the foresail may be attached to its stay. This may be done by means of special spring hanks, split rings, small shackles or a number of other nameless little thingummies which various owners have devised for the purpose. First secure the tack (the lower leading corner of the sail—usually this will have the maker's name stamped on it) with the shackle or other means provided; then hank the sail on to the forestay, starting with the bottom hank and working upwards. *Fireflies*, most *Merlin-Rockets* and *National* 12's hank the foresail on to its own halliard, which is led down from its block on the mast to the tack fitting on the bows of the dinghy. This reduces the sag to leeward of the foresail by half and, if there is no other method of tensioning the halliard, such as a winch or lever, is a good device. Generally a rope tail is spliced into the wire of such a halliard and this sometimes makes it a little difficult to hank the sail on,

Figure 4

as the splice will probably be too large to render through the hanks, as the sail goes up and the splice comes down. Figure 5 will indicate the arrangement of this type of halliard. Having hanked on the sail, make

SAIL-HANKED TO ITS OWN HALLIARD

ROPE TAIL

Figure 5

certain that it is not twisted and shackle on the halliard; (in the case of dinghies rigged in the manner just described, this will have to be done before the sail is hanked to the halliard.) The foresail sheets should then be put through the fairleads on the gunwale or deck. If there is more than one fairlead, ask your skipper which one to use. You should also ask if the sheets go outside, or inside, the shrouds—they will go outside in most cases, but there are a few exceptions. It has been found that the foresail sheets of *Cadets*, if rove through the shroud plates, are liable to chafe through the rigging lanyards and thereby cause the eventual downfall of the mast; it is preferable if this tendency be eliminated by leading the sheets through a large shackle secured to the shroud plate. Tie an overhand or figure-of-eight stopper knot in the end of the sheet, to prevent it being pulled back through the fairlead by the sail (see Figure 6). The mainsail can now be fixed to the boom, if it has been removed. In modern

dinghies, other than the *Cadet*, this will be done by inserting the bolt rope into the groove on the boom. The clew end of the foot of the sail is inserted into the boom groove at the end which pivots on the mast;

the clew can be recognized by the fact that the bolt rope ends at this corner in a whipping— the after edge or leech of the sail having no bolt rope and the top corner, or head, being

OVERHAND   FIGURE *of* EIGHT

Figure 6

distinguished by a metal or wooden headboard, whilst the tack will probably have the maker's name in it, as in the case of the foresail. When the sail has been pulled along the groove to the black band, a pin is inserted at the tack. The skipper will probably wish to fasten the clew, as, knowing the sail, he will be able to judge the right tension to be put on its edges.

The mainsail battens can now be inserted and tied in. These are usually numbered, but your skipper may wish to put in special ones to suit the conditions prevailing, and so ask him which he wishes to use. The batten pockets are situated on the after edge of the sail and there

A *National 12-footer* being expertly sailed. Note the position of the crew and helmsman when off the wind in light weather; also the light touch on tiller and sheets. Some helmsmen prefer to sit on the deck, with the crew on deck to leeward; they can then get a better view of the sails

In the *Hornet* class, the crew sits on a sliding plank which extends over the side of the boat. This is good fun and the increased leverage of the crew permits high speeds on a day like this

will be a piece of line, with two free ends, sewn to the sail itself, and two eyeletted holes in the pocket (see Figure 7). After putting the batten in its pocket, put the lines through the holes in the battens and then through the eyelets in the pocket and tie them together on the

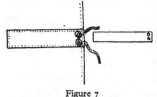

outside with a reef knot, not too tightly or you will crease the sail up. A better way than this is to make the knot come inside the pocket, by passing one of the lines through the hole in the batten, up through one eyelet, across the batten pocket on the outside and down through

Figure 7

the other eyelet to be tied to the second line, which is simply brought up through the hole in the batten ; this is neater, but most people will not bother to do it.

The mainsheet should now be shackled on to the end of the boom and to the stern of the dinghy. Sheets are the ropes which control the sails and are handled by the helmsman and crew when the boat is sailing. Some dinghies use double-purchase mainsheets and others single-purchase mainsheets ; most of them lead to the helmsman's hand from a block shackled on to the transom or the mainsheet horse on the stern of the dinghy, but there are exceptions. If you are in doubt about the proper arrangement of the mainsheet on his dinghy, ask the skipper and make certain before shackling it up. Generally a stopper knot will be put in the mainsheet a few feet from its end to prevent it running out through its blocks. Some helmsmen prefer not to have a mainsheet stopper knot when racing on rivers inland, when the sheet might get caught on an overhanging branch or other obstruction and stop the boat, for it would not be able to run out. Actually, the sheet is not very likely to run out in such a case anyway and so this secondary precaution is of doubtful value. An overhand knot is the best to use here, as it is neater than a figure-of-eight and, though liable to jam, should not ever have sufficient strain on it to make it do so.

The main halliard can now be shackled on and the skipper will, no doubt, assist in the hoisting of the sails. Usually, the sails will not be hoisted long before the dinghy is put afloat, except in very light weather, or when it is desired to air them. The boat will, as a rule, be turned and chocked head to wind before the sails are hoisted. When hoisting the mainsail, the luff bolt rope has to be fed into the groove on the after side of the mast and care should be taken to see that folds are not nipped into the slit from which the sail emerges ; if any such folds are present the sail must be lowered to get them out. Some dinghies are fitted with winches for the halliards ; the winch handle should be stowed away carefully after use, for it may be needed in an emergency. Many boats without halliard winches have a brass track screwed to the after side of the mast, on which the gooseneck fitting, to hold the boom, can slide up and down. In these boats, after the main halliard has been made fast, the gooseneck will be hauled downwards and fixed, either by a line made fast to a cleat, or by a pin or screw through the gooseneck fitting and into the track. The correct tension is thus put on the luff of the sail and this job will usually be done by the skipper.

The kicking strap, whose function is to hold the boom down on a reach or a run, when the wind tends to throw an excessive curve into the sail, lifting its foot and having a detrimental effect on its efficiency, should also be fixed in position and tightened up. One end of this will be found attached low down on the mast, or below it, near the bottom of the dinghy, and the other end is made fast to the underside of the boom about two feet from the mast. The skipper will put the correct tension on this tackle, if he intends it to be done before going afloat, but it is usually best to do this when the dinghy is actually sailing, as will be described a little later on in Chapter V.

It must not be supposed that the helmsman will all this time be sitting nearby in a deck-chair, sipping lemonade or something, whilst the crew carries out, unaided, all the tasks that have been mentioned. The fact is that the skipper will probably do the bulk of the jobs himself, but it is necessary for the crew to know how to do them, hence the indication of the correct method in this chapter.

The crew should now carefully check over the gear in the boat and see that all that will be needed is aboard. If the weather is light, or the wind likely to ease off during the course of the race, a kedge anchor should be carried ; the skipper will make the final decision on whether to take this, but he may need reminding. Do this in plenty of time, as it may even be necessary to add greater length of line to the anchor, if the dinghy is being raced in water deeper than that in which she usually sails. The anchor cable is frequently wound up on a cable drum, which keeps it tidy, but if this is not so on your boat, see that the line is coiled down carefully, without kinks, and stow it away very neatly, but so as to be easily accessible. Opinions differ over anchors and there are many different types in use. It is suggested, however, that, whatever the type, it should be made up ready for use at a moment's notice and not be left in a folded condition, if it is of a collapsible pattern. A bailer and sponge should also be aboard, though sponges are a luxury in which it is not always possible to indulge, these days. A paddle should be stowed within the crew's reach—it may be needed as soon as the boat is put afloat. It will, of course, not be needed during a race and so should be put well out of the way after the five minutes' warning gun before the start. Do not stow things right up in the bows of a racing dinghy, as this will upset her fore and aft trim, but put them as near amidships as you can without them getting in your way. Most of the gear will have to be stowed about as far forward as the mast.

In the case of dinghies carrying spinnakers, the skipper will choose the correct one to take and will show you where to stow it. It will usually go in a net under the deck, in boats with decks, and in a light box or canvas bag attached to the mast thwart in open dinghies. See that the headboard of the sail is handy for clipping on to the halliard; Englefield signal halliard clips are often used for this job and the

method of fastening them is shown in Figure 8— the slot of one part is slid into the slot of the other at right angles. The spinnaker sheets or guys should be coiled down carefully and stowed so that they will have no kinks or knots if the sail is needed. The spinnaker boom should be aboard and handy, or, in boats without spinnakers, the jib stick should be carried and you should make certain of the correct way to fix it to the clew of the foresail and to the mast. The rudder and tiller, with a pin to keep the latter into the rudder head, should be placed in the after end of the dinghy. Buoyancy bags should be checked for air pressure, or buoyancy tanks looked over to ensure that their plugs are in position and firmly so. Draining plugs, if there are any in the bottom or transom of the boat, must also

Figure 8

be secured firmly in place; it has been known for dinghies to be put afloat and sailed away from the shore with the plugs out—to the shame and discomfort of her crew and derisive peals of mirth from the onlookers. Racing flags with halliards should be hoisted early, so that the latter may dry out and stretch; when they have done this they should be tautened so that the little flag mast stands up jauntily and does not flop about like a tired inebriate. You should also familiarize yourself with the working of the centreboard hoist; winches are used in some of the larger dinghies, whilst others just use a simple purchase; in the case of many *National* 12's the tackle will be led to both sides of the boat to facilitate the handling of it when on either tack.

The dinghy now being ready for the water, you should, if time and opportunity permit, make yourself acquainted with the course to be sailed. For one thing, this will increase your interest in the race and, secondly, the skipper may need your reassurance as to the whereabouts of the next mark, if he is himself unfamiliar with the water. It will also be helpful if you can synchronize your watch with that to be used by the starter and, if you are sailing on tidal water, ascertain and remember the times of low and high water and the commencement and cessation of the ebb and flow.

A few helmsmen prefer the crew to take the times of the preliminary warning guns and the starting gun of a race, but most of them will like to do this for themselves. The general practice followed in the starting of races may here be explained with advantage. A signal flag, indicating the class to be started, is hoisted ten minutes before the start and a gun fired at the same time to draw attention to the signal; five minutes later another gun is fired and the code flag "P" (the familiar Blue Peter—a white rectangle on a blue ground), is hoisted to join the class flag; exactly five minutes later the starting gun is fired and both flags are lowered. In actual fact, the object of the guns is merely to draw the attention of the competitors to the lowering or hoisting of the flags, but, in dinghy racing, it is often impossible to watch or even see these, and so the guns are taken as the indication of the start. Remember, if you are doing this timing, that sound travels rather slowly—it takes five seconds to go a mile—so allow for this when giving the time in a race in which you are starting some distance from the guns, for a few seconds at the start may be vital in big fleets, when the consequences of being blanketed from the wind by a hoard of other dinghies are serious. You should start the stopwatch as soon as you hear the ten-minute gun—it may catch you unawares, but it is not vital to get the time exactly. The watch should be stopped at least thirty seconds before you estimate the five-minute gun will go off and it should be returned to zero and the skipper warned, so that he will not make any complicated manoeuvre which will involve you and distract your attention; for the watch must be started with the signal. If you can see the smoke from the gun or the signal flag, so much the better—do not wait for the sound to reach you. Usually you will give the helmsman warning of each minute to go between the five-minute gun and the start, then the last half minute, quarter minute, ten seconds, and then each second to the "off." Even if the skipper does his own timing, it is a good thing for you to do a check, so that, if anything goes wrong with his watch he will not be quite ignorant of when to start.

CHAPTER IV

CREWING (2)—GETTING AFLOAT AND ASHORE

Moving dinghies—Lifting a dinghy—Trolleys—Launching—Getting aboard
—Leaving and approaching the shore — Getting the dinghy ashore —
Unrigging—Care of sails—Hosing down and leathering off—Stowing—
Sharing the duties with skipper

DINGHIES are generally either lifted up and carried to the water or are put on small-wheeled trolleys specially made for the job of moving dinghies. Sometimes the trolley will be run right into the water until the dinghy floats off it.

Like most other things to do with boats, there is a right and a wrong way to lift a dinghy and damage can frequently be done by clumsy manhandling. You will not immediately find your way to the heart of an owner upon whose dinghy you pounce with well-meaning but misguided violence, ultimately staggering back clutching only a small and vital piece of timber. Keen observation—which is one of the most valuable attributes a dinghy racer can have—will quickly show you which parts of the dinghy it is best to lift her by. If you are not sure at first sight, ask the owner, for you may otherwise get hold of something that has been put into the boat to withstand a downward strain and not a tough upward pull. *National* 12's are the trickiest from this point of view. Some dinghies—*Merlins* and a few *National* 12's—have handles on each side by which to lift them; one person on each and another lifting the bows can fairly easily carry a dinghy of these classes. *Fireflies* have four short rope lanyards protruding through the deck by which they may be lifted and they will then be managed quite easily with a fifth hand under the bows. *International* 14-*footers* are a bit heavier but are easy to get hold of, as, being quite undecked, the gun-wales afford excellent hand-holds. *Swordfish* and 18-*foot Nationals* require more than five for a comfortable lift, the latter really needing nine or more to manage her 7½ or 8 hundredweights, whilst the former, at about 430 pounds, can be managed by seven.

When putting a dinghy on to a trolley it is important to see that the latter is about midway between the bow and stern, so that the boat is properly balanced, and that the keel is in the centre of the trolley and square to its axle, otherwise the dinghy will travel along crabwise and be very hard to manoeuvre in restricted spaces. Two people can load a dinghy, other than an 18-*footer*, on to a trolley. Sometimes a dinghy will be seen being dragged along on her keel; this does not do so much damage as might be imagined from the frightful scraping noises that are created, for she is to a certain extent protected by her metal keel-band; but it is far better if it can be avoided.

Dinghies are launched bow or stern first, the direction of the wind usually being the deciding factor. Those with open tiller ports are liable to ship water through them and care should be taken to avoid this; one frequently finishes a race with water aboard, but it is annoying to start in that state. When launching an already rigged boat, a watch should be kept to see that the boom does not blow about and get caught in the rigging of other dinghies, and she should be kept upright to avoid the possibility of the mast fouling others. It is surprising how easy it is to forget about what is happening to the mast when man-handling a dinghy and it is not unknown for telephone wires to suffer; the writer has twice witnessed the downfall of the wireless aerial of a famous West Country yacht club on the occasion of visits by *National* 12's to open races run under the flag of that Club.

These simple points may seem very obvious, but they are neverthe-less sometimes overlooked, with consequent damage to boats, gear and nerves which is far better avoided.

In most cases, dinghies have to be launched from slipways or beaches, and it is therefore frequently necessary to stand in the water before getting aboard. This means getting wet feet at the outset, but unfortunately cannot be avoided. As the dinghy becomes waterborne, try to hold her head to wind. The skipper may ask you to get aboard, first; sit forward of the centrethwart and in the centre of the boat unless you are asked to fit the rudder and tiller, in which case you will have to come aft (don't forget to insert the retaining pin which keeps the tiller into the rudder head). You may be asked to lower a little centreplate before the skipper climbs aboard and you should have the paddle handy. When the skipper is aboard, he will have to get the rudder and tiller fixed as soon as the dinghy is in deep enough water—if this has not already been done by the crew; until this is done, you should be ready to paddle to keep the dinghy clear of others and should warn the skipper if you are getting too close to any obstruction—he will probably be leaning over the transom, trying to fix the rudder, and will not be able to see where he is going. It may be necessary to back the foresail in order to get the boat's head to pay off the leeward so that she can commence to sail. If you are asked to do this, it is done by holding the foresail up to the windward side, as in Figure 9. As soon as the dinghy's head is far enough off the wind for your sail to draw properly on the leeward side, you should let it come across.

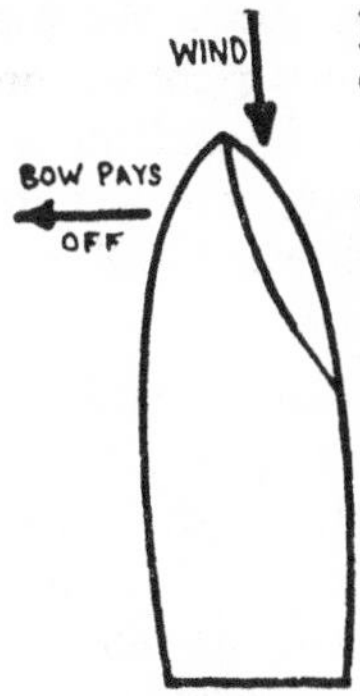

WIND

BOW PAYS
OFF

Figure 9

The sailing of the dinghy, from the crew's point of view, will be dealt with in the next chapter, so let us presume that, both helmsman and crew having done everything that they ought to sail the boat at her best speed, they are now returning victorious to the shore and tea, whilst the club steward prepares supper for their rivals, whose dinghies' sails are still but little specks of white on the horizon.

If the wind is offshore, it will be possible to sail in without lowering any canvas. As the shore is approached, the skipper will probably tell you to ease your foresail sheets and he will bring in the dinghy with only the mainsail drawing. You should be prepared to raise the centreboard completely as the dinghy reaches shallow water and should jump out of the boat before she touches the ground if possible ; go early enough, but not too soon, especially on a steeply shelving shore—the writer's crew once jumped a little early and completely disappeared from sight into about seven feet of water! Use your own discretion when to go, as the skipper will be busy removing the tiller and rudder as you enter shallow water. Hold the dinghy head to wind ; if there is more than a light breeze, the skipper will probably lower the sails and remove the boom from the gooseneck before you get the boat ashore. Collect the foresail as it comes down and do not let it blow into the water.

If the wind is onshore things are not quite so easy and the skipper will most likely decide to lower the mainsail and sail in under the foresail only. He may also make the same decision if the wind is very strong and there is some distance to be sailed from the finishing line to the place where the dinghy is to be brought ashore, even if this shore is a windward one. If he decides on this plan he will luff the boat as near as possible head to wind, while you lower the mainsail. Before he does this, you can ease the boom downhaul, if there is one, and uncleat the main halliard or fit the winch handle. As the boat is luffed, you can haul the foresail sheet and this may be held by the skipper or roughly cleated by you or, preferably, you can jam it between your foot and the floorboards. Let the halliard go and haul on the luff bolt rope of the sail, which you should get down as quickly as possible, seeing that the boom comes down within the boat and not over the side. Take the boom from the gooseneck and tuck it under the deck mast or thwart—this will bring its far end inside the transom and it will then lie on the centrethwart and give clearance for the movement of the tiller; also remove the winch handle, before the foresheets get snarled up on it and perhaps jerk it over the side. You can then handle the foresheets once again and the helmsman will bear away. As you approach the shore, you will have to let your foresheets right out or, possibly, lower the foresail if the skipper thinks she will come in too fast; but the centreboard will not be needed on the way in if you are running free and this can be raised in plenty of time, which will give you a better opportunity to attend to the foresail.

Occasionally you may be called upon to pick up a mooring. The mooring may be approached in a variety of manners according to the conditions of wind and tide; this side of the procedure is dealt with in Chapter VIII. You should have the paddle handy just in case it is needed to bring the boat up to the buoy. In the smaller decked dinghies the skipper will probably aim to bring the mooring alongside on the shoulder of the bow of his boat—just ahead of the main shrouds. It may be safe to wriggle yourself forward on the foredeck of one of the larger dinghies or go forward of the mast in an open 14-*footer*, but care should always be taken when doing this as your weight will depress the bows and lift the stern, thereby substantially decreasing the stability of the dinghy. The skipper should indicate his intentions to you and tell you if he wishes the float or buoy of the mooring brought aboard; alternatively, he may decide that it is better to make fast to the buoy itself.

If you bring the float aboard be careful not to scrape it up the side of the hull. Get it in ahead of the shrouds, lift it aft and put in the bottom of the boat, keeping it clear of any lowered sails. The easiest way to make it fast will probably be to take a few turns with a sheet or centreboard tackle round the centrethwart, then form a loop in the buoy rope and make your light rope fast to this with a sheet bend. Alternatively, you can take a long bight from your anchor line and use

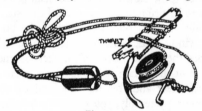

this, as in the diagrammatic representation in Figure 10. If there is no fairlead for a mooring rope near the stem of the dinghy, the mooring rope should be stopped up to the forestay or foresail tack fitting with a light line to

Figure 10

keep it in the bows and prevent it sliding back and forth on the gunwale and causing chafe. Needless to say, the stopping line just mentioned and the sheet, tackle or bight of anchor line to be used for securing to the mooring should be made fast in readiness before the mooring is picked up, so that the operation may be completed quickly.

If you are going to secure to the buoy without getting it aboard, have the line with which you are securing already made fast—it can even be stopped down to the forestay in advance, but be certain that you leave a very ample length of slack with which to operate while you make fast to the buoy. A round turn and two half hitches, shown on the

anchor ring in Figure 11, will do to secure the dinghy to the loop of the buoy. If you are using a bight from the dinghy's anchor cable the following is a very quick method of making fast. Take a very long bight—about three times the length needed if you were to secure

Figure 11

with a hitch to the buoy direct. Pass this bight through the loop of the buoy and bring it back on board. Now take a turn round one of the flukes of the anchor, pass the end of the bight across the shank and hook it under the other fluke. Figure 11 explains this method.

If the dinghy is to be brought ashore and there is a launching trolley available, this will be used to get her out. The trolley is pushed well down into the water and the boat floated over it, both being pulled ashore together, so that the dinghy becomes trolleyborne as the trolley rises under her. If no trolley is available, there will usually be helping hands to assist in getting the boat ashore. In either case, the draining plugs, if fitted, should be removed as soon as the boat is clear of the water. Thus there will be less weight to lift and the water will run out more easily when she is on the slope of the shore than it will when she is brought on to level ground, where she will be chocked-up and unrigged.

The battens should then be removed from the mainsail. When doing this, take care to see that the sail does not fall into the wet bilge and get saturated. When the mainsail has been removed from the boom and the foresail unhanked and unshackled, they can be folded and put in the sail bag if they are quite dry. Foresail sheets should never be put in the bag, but should be coiled down and left outside, as they usually get wet when in use and retain moisture for a long time. If the sails have been at all wetted with spray, they should be allowed to dry before being bagged, providing that you have been sailing on fresh water. If the spray was salt, they must be rinsed off with fresh water and dried—any salt remaining on the sail would absorb moisture when the air is damp and the sail would become clammy or quite wet, even though stowed, when dry, in a canvas bag. A race frequently finishes with a run or reach off the wind, on which the sails, which may have become wet when going to windward, dry out; in that case, if you are not sure whether the sails have salt in them, the best method of finding out is to taste them—they are most likely to be affected along the foot of the foresail and the tack of the mainsail.

Having got the sails out of the way, the hull should, if it has been in salt water and is to be kept in the best possible condition, be hosed down with fresh water. A stirrup pump is ideal for this job and one bucketful of water will be all that is needed if the fine spray is used. The inside of the centreplate case should also be rinsed out and, of course, the rudder should not be forgotten, whilst anything else likely to be affected by salt water, such as blocks, rigging screws, sheets and canvas toe-straps, should be given a squirt. Most of the surplus moisture can be wiped off with a sponge and then the outside of the hull dried off and polished with a wash-leather. This is all rather a labour of love and may be considered by some helmsmen a little too much work to be carried out as a routine, but a good finish demands much hard work with sandpaper and the careful application of paint or varnish, and it will stand a better chance of remaining good and saving hard labour of this kind later if it is kept in the best possible condition by tender care when the boat is brought ashore.

The mainsheet should be coiled down in a large coil, as this will dry out more easily than a smaller one. The battens should be stowed on a flat surface, so that there is no chance of them getting warped. If the mast is to remain up and there are flag halliards, the racing pennant should be lowered. All the halliards should be stopped down fairly taut with a length of twine passed through the shackles. It is a good idea to pass a line round the shrouds and the halliards, to pull the latter clear of the mast and thus prevent them chafing it when they are blown about in the wind. If the mast has to be removed, tension will first have to be taken off the shrouds and forestay ; if the rigging screws are unscrewed completely, see that the body is screwed back several complete turns on to one of the ends, so as to prevent it from getting lost.

Having tidied up any loose gear, covered the boat and seen that she is securely chocked upright, you may then retire to the comfort of the clubhouse and do justice to your tea, in the pleasant knowledge that you have done all for your skipper's boat that even the most fastidious of dinghies could wish for. It may well seem that this chapter and the previous one comprise a frightening list of duties, but it should be remembered that, in fact, two people are carrying out most of them— the crew and the helmsman—and, in practice it does not take very long. The author has taken a dinghy from a boathouse one minute before the ten-minute gun of a race, got the mast from its rack in another shed, rigged the dinghy and got her afloat and sailing before the five-minute gun; at one moment she was sitting disconsolately under her covers indoors, sulking because she thought that she was going to miss a race, and six minutes later she was romping about on the water aching to get started. This is not a practice to be recommended, but it does show that, with experience, most of the jobs enumerated in this chapter can be carried out in a very short time.

CHAPTER V

CREWING (3)—MAINLY ON SAIL TRIMMING

Psychological survey—Points of sailing—Tacking—Starboard tack, right of way—Action of sails to windward—Real and apparent wind—Trim—The flow of sails—Effects of light weather—Technique to windward—Effects of rough water—Goosewinging the foresail—Spinnakers—Changing tack—Sliding seats—Trapezes

BEFORE getting down to the real job of sailing a dinghy, it would perhaps be wise to dabble in a little elementary psychology in relation to your helmsman; it may be a trifle tedious, but it is nevertheless important.

One of the first things to which a good crew should try to adapt himself as soon as possible is the character of his skipper, for his attitude towards life in general may appear to alter once he is afloat. That may sound a little ominous, but what is meant is this: many helmsmen take their racing very seriously and the stress on their nerves is considerable. This may affect them in a number of ways, for many assume the outward veneer of perfect calm, which probably covers an extremely high pitch of nervous tuning, whilst the nervous energy of others, which has been summoned for the fray, may overflow in a stream of invective against boats, competitors, the wind, water and everything else, including—I hate to tell you, gentle reader—*crews*. Whatever is the habit of your helmsman, you must accustom yourself to it. It is not pleasant to be called a ham-fisted oaf, but allowances have to be made or else the situation becomes impossible and the working of the boat must cease whilst apologies are handed out all round. The great thing to remember is that although this may be rather depressing, unpleasant and annoying, it is not really meant and you must just adopt a thick-skinned attitude, which is not injured by wild words. It must certainly not be thought that all helmsmen are inclined to nag whilst racing, for this would be very far from the truth; but one feels that this warning is necessary, in order that the novice may not be upset if he is unlucky enough to be at the receiving end of such treatment on his first sail—it is not to be taken seriously and is just a safety valve adopted by some and, as such, should be generally and generously ignored.

If there are no such outbursts and an air of perfect calm emanates from your skipper, you should nevertheless hesitate to assume that he is necessarily as calm and as confident as he appears. His orders, though quietly given, should be carried out no less promptly than if they were snapped at you. You will find, in any case, that orders are given and not requests made, for there just is not the time for "please" and "thank you" during a dinghy race.

An experienced helmsman will usually try to explain to you a little of what his tactics are and the object behind his strategy. This is not to invite your comments, but so that you may have a better idea of what to expect when orders have to be given. As a rule you should not speak more than is necessary to the skipper during a race, for his powers of concentration should be left free to cope with the exacting task of getting his dinghy along faster than his rivals—so should yours—and he has not the mental energy to spare for chit-chat.

Figure 12

Now for the sailing. It is presumed that the reader understands the elements of sailing already, but it is essential that a little space be devoted towards making certain of a few points.

When you sail from one place to another you will have to do one of four things—tack, beat, reach or run—dependent on your course in relation to the wind. Each of the points of sailing, as they are called, has its own difficulties and techniques, and although the inexperienced may at first consider one less important and easier than the next, he will in time find that all are equally important and that the technique to be applied to each is just as intriguingly hard to master as it is for the others.

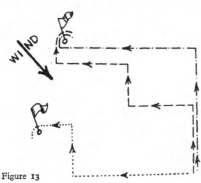

Figure 13

A racing dinghy can sail at an angle of about 45° to the wind. Therefore, in still water, a dinghy will be able to sail direct to any mark which is more than 45° on either side of the wind direction (see Figure 12); to sail to any point which is less than 45° on either side of the wind direction, the dinghy will not be able to proceed direct, but will have to tack (see Figure 13). On open currentless water, there is no particular point at which the course should be altered and the boat sailed on the other tack, and, as will be seen in Figure 13, long or short tacks may be made. In actual practice, there is usually some factor, such as the consideration of wind strength, current or the position of other competitors, which decides when the tacks should be made. A boat is said to be on the port tack when the wind is coming over her port side—her sails are therefore to starboard; when the sails are to port, the boat is, of course, on the starboard tack. It is most important to remember that under the R.Y.A. racing rules and also the rule of the road at sea, which applies to all vessels afloat, boats on the starboard tack have right of way over boats on the port tack. It is sometimes a little difficult to remember which tack you are on at first, but you will know almost instinctively and without thinking as you gain experience. The writer used to remember it in this way when he first learnt to race: being right-handed, he was perhaps at some slight advantage when steering with this hand; this would be on the port tack and when he was sitting in the helmsman's normal position to

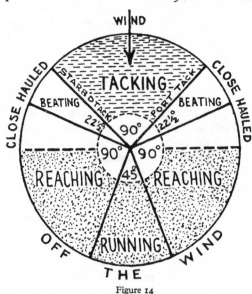

Figure 14

windward; it seemed only fair, therefore, when steering with the right hand to give the advantage of right of way to those who were steering with the left hand, i.e. on the starboard tack (this was not a very logical reasoning, but served its purpose and might do the same for others).

The divisions between beating, reaching and running are not clear cut, but Figure 14 gives a rough indication which will be sufficiently definite for the purposes of studying the handling of a dinghy on these various points of sailing. The sketch referred to shows what any boat, starting from the centre of the circle, would be doing when proceeding to any point on the circumference of the circle; if she is going to any point above the pecked diameter line of the circle, she will be going to windward, or be on the wind.

One of the fundamental essentials which must be grasped when learning to race is the correct trimming of the sails. The proper angle of the sail to the wind direction is, of course, of paramount importance, especially in the case of the foresail, for the incorrect sheeting of this sail will completely upset the efficiency of the mainsail. In order to understand the action of the sails when working to windward, let us try to illustrate what is happening.

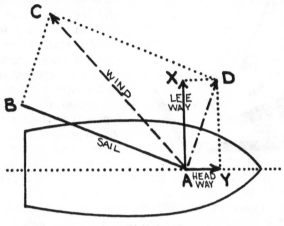

Figure 15

The whole thing is represented diagrammatically in Figure 15, which shows a boat on the starboard tack : the sail is represented by the line AB, whilst the wind is represented in direction and strength by the line AC. Now AC may be resolved into two component forces, according to the rule of the parallelogram of forces, and this gives one component which acts parallel to and along the sail without producing any effect and which may therefore be ignored, and the second component, which is smaller, and acts at right angles to the sail. This component AD can be further resolved into two more components, AX, which is the larger and causes the tendency towards leeway, and AY, the smaller, which produces

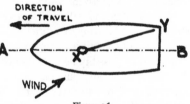

Figure 16

headway. Since leeway is to a great extent prevented by the centreboard and the lateral resistance of the hull, to which we will refer later, the forward motion is the only one which remains and acts upon the dinghy.

The same thing can be demonstrated, rather less technically, with the aid of a piece of soap and a mirror or some other flat surface, by a method which the writer devised some years ago. Referring to Figure 16, the lateral resistance of the boat is represented by the line AB—a wall of water particles against which the hull, centreboard and rudder may push, but cannot pass ; the trim of the sail is shown by

XY. Now with the assistance of our mirror, a wedge-shaped slice of soap and a slippery forefinger, the essentials in Figure 16 may be

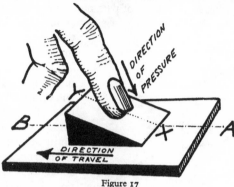

translated into a working model, as in Figure 17. The lateral resistance in this case is afforded by the mirror, while the angle of trim of the sail is represented by the sloping surface of the soap; the whole apparatus is made wet and slippery and the "wind" applied with a forefinger, when the

Figure 17

soap will skid along the mirror in the direction shown. Maybe if you have already tried this experiment in your bath, though not in the voluntary pursuit of scientific knowledge, by sitting on the soap, you may recall that you perhaps went one way, whilst the soap went the other. In this way you will see that the wind really "squeezes" your dinghy to windward and you will quickly see what happens if you try to "pinch" your boat too close to the wind, with her sails sheeted very hard in, if you cut your wedge of soap very thin and apply your wind-finger to this at a very small angle.

The best and most dependable guide to the wind direction as it affects the dinghy that you are sailing in, is provided by the racing flag or burgee at the top of the mast. In many places even this cannot be relied upon, because the wind is so cut up by trees, buildings and other obstructions that it may well be blowing in a different direction at the head of the sail from its direction at the foot. It may possibly be read elsewhere that the flag gives only an indication of the apparent, and not the true, wind direction; but since it is the direction of the apparent wind which concerns the driving of the dinghy, it is quite false to say that the flag

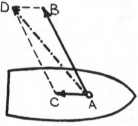

Figure 18

gives no reliable guide to the correct trimming of the sail, especially when the boat is off the wind. An explanation of the meaning of the term "apparent wind" will be understood with the aid of Figure 18. Let the true wind direction and strength be represented in this sketch by the line AB; now the wind caused by the dinghy's forward motion will be equal and opposite to the latter and is represented in this case by the line AC; the apparent wind will therefore be represented by the line AD and will be seen to come more ahead and be slightly stronger than the real wind. A strong tide will also affect the apparent direction or force of the wind. It will not be out of place to mention here that, when a strong puff of wind hits a dinghy's sails, it will apparently come freer and the dinghy can therefore be luffed a little and still kept sailing hard. The reason for this is that the speed of the wind has increased more quickly than the boat can accelerate and, therefore, in Figure 18, AB has increased in length (i.e. strength) whilst AC has remained about the same.

As a very rough and ready rule, the angle between the general plane of the sails and the centreline of the dinghy should be kept just within the angle, say 10° less, which the flag makes with the centreline, as in Figure 19. This is only an approximate guide, however, and experience alone can determine the absolutely correct trim. Generally speaking, when you are tacking in a dinghy the foresail sheet will be hauled in as hard as possible and held there. It is most important that the foresail be kept at the same angle of trim when the boat is being sailed as close to the wind as possible, because the experienced helmsman will watch the foresail and steer his boat by the appearance of this sail. If the luff of the sail "lifts" a little and has the appearance of being starved of wind, he will bear away somewhat until it is just "drawing" properly and he will try always to keep the boat heading so that the foresail is just at this angle to the wind—just drawing at the luff. Obviously, if you do not keep the sail in properly or if you alter the trim, he will not be able to steer his boat to the best advantage.

WIND

Figure 19

It will of course be immediately apparent to you that the sails actually assume a curve, when they are filled with wind, and are not a flat surface as shown in the earlier sketches in this chapter. This curve is purposely put into the sail when it is made, because, as in the case of an aeroplane wing, there is more pull or lift from a curved surface than there is from a flat one. Strange as it may seem, the most power developed from the wind is produced by a pull or suction of negative pressure on the leeward side of the sails. Figure 20 will, it is hoped, illustrate this point, by showing the approximate course of the wind-stream over the sails of a normally-rigged dinghy. The section on the leeward side of a sail and the advantage gained by having a sail with a certain amount of curve or belly in it, can be easily demonstrated by a simple experiment with a piece of paper. Thus: fold a piece of stiffish paper down the centre, dividing it into two; now cut down the fold in two places so as to leave three hinges on which the two halves may pivot; cut one half roughly to the shape of a dinghy mainsail.

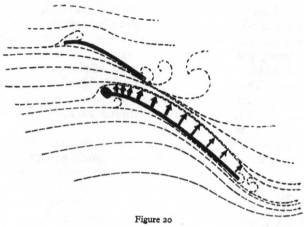

Figure 20

Hold the other half with its surface horizontal and level with your mouth—the part representing the sail will hang down somewhat from its own weight. Now blow across the top of the horizontal surface, representing the flow of air to the leeward side of the sail, and the other half will rise up—even above the horizontal. Blow along the under surface, representing the windward side of the sail, and the hinged part will rise up only until it is just below the horizontal. Now, if the free half is curved in the manner of a good sail, it will rise much further under the influence of a stream of air over the surface representing the leeward side of the sail, showing that there is increased lift or suction from the correctly curved shape—the curve is called the flow or belly of the sail. Figure 21 shows how the paper is cut and folded for the simple experiment just described.

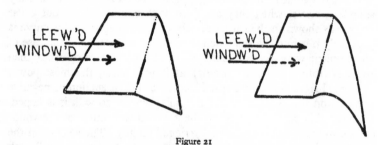

Figure 21

This should make it quite clear that if the foresail is incorrectly trimmed, it may upset the flow of wind on the lee side of the sail and thus reduce the all-important suction effect. It will therefore be noted that, from this point of view as well, the foresheet hand has a great responsibility.

The flow of the foresail is produced partly as a result of the slight sagging off to leeward of the luff of the sail and in very light weather this is reduced, so that if the sail is hauled in taut by the sheet, it is flattened and very little curve remains in it. It is in this light weather, however, when the speed of the wind over the sails is very low, that we need most flow, and therefore the skipper, who should know this, may decide to ease the sheets a little, even if it means that he must bear away a trifle in order that the sails may work with maximum efficiency. If you consider the wings of various types of aircraft, you will realize that those designed for low speeds—such as gliders—have wings of a deep chord, whilst the wings of high-speed aeroplanes usually have

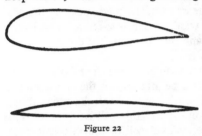

a much thinner section, as will be seen in the comparison of the two wing sections shown in Figure 22, the upper one being of the glider type whilst the lower one is similar to those used on high-speed aircraft.

Figure 22

When sailing as close to the wind as possible, then, you haul in as hard as you like on the foresail, except in light airs, when you may ease the sheet a trifle to put more flow into the sail.

One of the main points to remember when racing a dinghy is that as a general rule when working to windward, the boat's course is altered to meet alterations in wind direction, so that in places where the wind is interfered with by buildings and trees, the dinghy is constantly luffing and bearing away a little, so as to work as close to the wind as possible and keep going with the sails full and drawing. Off the wind, however, the course is kept more or less steady and it is the trim of the sails that is altered to meet shifts in wind direction. As with most generalizations, there are exceptions to this rule, but they are beyond the scope of this book, except that mention must be made of the fact that in exceptionally heavy puffs it may be necessary to ease the foresail in order to prevent a capsize. This is only done as a last resort and it should certainly not be eased without an order from the helmsman, because in strong blows much of the wind may be "spilt" out of the mainsail by easing the mainsheet and the boat being sailed along very largely on the foresail only; if the foresail is eased too soon, the dinghy will lose way and may become out of control.

Undoubtedly the skipper will at first tell you when the foresail should be eased a little and when it should be hauled, but with practice you should be able to judge for yourself. It will be quite obvious when the sail is not properly full of wind, because a small area near the luff will look crinkly and not stretched out taut by the breeze. When it appears thus, haul in on your sheet a little until the wrinkles just disappear; you will probably not need to haul in much. Remember that when the skipper says, "Ease your sheet a little," "Haul it a little," he really does mean a *little*; let it out slowly—half an inch on the sheet may mean the difference between a properly drawing sail and one that is not working to its utmost. When sailing in a bit of a lop at sea, you will notice that as the dinghy slithers sideways down a wave, the luff of the foresail may lift and show the signs already mentioned of not being filled; the sheet should then be hauled a little to cure this situation. It is possible that your helmsman is allowing the dinghy to deviate from her course slightly with each wave, but, even though a perfectly constant course may be sailed, the effect of the waves pushing the boat sideways, directly away from the wind, is such as to reduce the effective speed of the wind on your sails and thereby bring the direction of the apparent wind to slightly more ahead.

Off the wind, the trim of the mainsail and the racing flag should be your guide, though you should still be attentive to the appearance of your sail as well. If the foresail is hauled in too hard, the mainsail may be backwinded by the airflow from it and this will be quite obvious from the fact that the luff of the mainsail will be blown considerably to windward. This will, of course, happen when the mainsail has to be eased by the skipper in a heavy puff to keep the dinghy from heeling too much and all you can do to prevent this is to sit out even harder. In some dinghies, with large foresails and a lot of flow in the mainsail, the latter may be backwinded almost all the time by the foresail and this cannot be avoided by the crew. Perhaps the best way of judging when the sail is doing its work most efficiently is to ease it until the crinkles just appear at the luff and then haul it again so that they just disappear, when the sail will be properly trimmed.

When running before the wind, it may be possible to trim the foresail on the opposite side to the mainsail. So long as the sail is pulling well on the same side do not disturb it, but as soon as it ceases to work you should tell your skipper and, if he thinks fit, he may tell you to get it across to the other side or to "goosewing" it. In order for it to set properly when goosewinged, it is essential to free plenty of sheet from the side on which the sail was previously working. As a rule, the skipper will hold the new working sheet, as the sail will draw better if this is held well aft. If the wind is steady and the run a long one, the skipper may decide to use the jib stick, which facilitates the better drawing of the foresail before the wind. To fit this, grasp the sheets and get hold of the clew of the sail; fix the jib stick to the clew by whatever method of attachment is provided, taking care that the sail is not twisted; push the sail out by means of the stick and fix the latter to the mast. The jib stick must be fastened to the mast as soon as possible, as it is against the racing rules to use it unattached and held in the hand or fixed to the shrouds or hull. When getting it in, the reverse of the above process is followed, and when gybing it may only be necessary to remove the jib stick from the mast and swing it upwards and over to the other side with the sail still attached, fixing it to the mast again on the fresh side.

Spinnakers require a lot of practice before they can be set quickly and efficiently. It is not intended to give a detailed description here, for techniques differ widely and are often dictated by the arrangements made for the stowing of the sail when not in use. Frequently the spinnaker of an *International 14-footer* is set ahead of the forestay and the foresail lowered; to do this quickly and without slowing the boat up during the operation is quite a tricky business. *Merlin-Rockets* are not permitted to sheet their spinnakers around the forestay and the foresail is not lowered.

The procedure outlined here should serve as a rough guide; skippers and crews will almost certainly wish to settle between themselves their own individual way of doing the job. The sail is generally stowed in a drawer under the foredeck or a net or canvas bag. Sometimes the sheets can be rove through fairleads and cleated in approximately the right positions before the sail is hoisted, but this is not always advisable as it may mean that the sail fills with wind as it is being hoisted and it may do so in such a way that it is difficult to hoist or that it is twisted so that the sheets are found to be made fast on the wrong sides of the boat. The halliard should be clipped on and quite clear; the spinnaker boom ready for use. Sometimes it will be found easier if the helmsman does the hoisting—there is no need for him to hold the mainsheet when running, as the boom will usually be squared off against the shrouds—while the crew sees that the sail goes up properly and attaches the spinnaker boom as soon as it is hoisted, taking care to see that the sheets do not get loose and fly forward as the sail goes up and as a rule passing the weather sheet outside the weather shrouds and to the helmsman as soon as the spinnaker boom is in place. When lowering the spinnaker, the spinnaker boom is first removed, the halliard is then let go and the crew muffles the sail and hauls it down as quickly as possible, stuffing it back into its stowage place as neatly as he can.

When gybing with a spinnaker, the mainsail will first be allowed to come over. The spinnaker boom is then detached from the mast and that end of it is then attached to new weather clew of the sail, so that the boom is attached to both clews of the sail and spans its foot. The sail is then pushed across to the weather side of the boat by means of the spinnaker boom and the leeward clew of the spinnaker is then detached from the boom, which is fixed to the mast.

When approaching a mark at which you know that the spinnaker will have to come down, leave it up as long as possible, of course, but it is always better to get it down a little early rather than leaving it too late and getting it wrapped up on the mast spreaders when the boat turns on the wind.

When changing from one tack to the other, you will quickly find the easiest and best way of managing your sail. The helmsman will usually be able to give you plenty of warning before actually tacking the boat, but when racing in very close company, or in confined or shallow waters, this may not be altogether possible. Ideally, it is best if the skipper can give a preliminary warning about ten seconds before the tack is made and then another one just as he is about to put the helm down and turn the dinghy. The warnings he will give will probably be, " Ready about," " Lee-oh," but sometimes all the warning that he will be able to give you will be, "About"—and the dinghy will be turned as it is said. It is absolutely essential, therefore, to keep your sheets tidied and clear all the time and after tacking you should make certain that they are in this condition as soon as possible.

Every good crew will develop his own technique, which may well be better than the method which follows, but this will give some idea to complete novices of what to do when the boat is tacked. Let us assume that you are sitting out on the starboard gunwale—the dinghy being on the starboard tack; all your sheets are, of course, clear and you are quite ready when the skipper says, " Lee-oh," and the dinghy begins to turn—she will spin round very quickly. As she begins to turn, leave go of the old working sheet—the one that goes through the port fair-lead—and grasp the other in your left hand, put your right leg over

the centreboard case and, as the boat passes the eye of the wind, move your body across to the other side, using your right hand to free the old working sheet from the port fairlead ; then turn round and face the centre of the boat, sit on the gunwale and haul the new working sheet. In this method the crew faces aft, not forward, as he changes his position from one gunwale to the other. He thus avoids getting his head caught up in the kicking strap (see pages 32, 61, 62). All this will be done quite automatically after a little while. Never allow the old working sheet—the one which goes through the fairlead on the side which is to windward on the new tack—to become taut and to act on

Figure 23   the foresail in the slightest degree, as it will pull the sail to windward and cause it to set improperly. In very light airs, off the wind, even the weight of the sheets may be sufficient to upset the proper setting of the foresail and, in this case, the crew may be asked to hold the sheets upwards and outwards somewhat from the dinghy in order to overcome this tendency; on no account should the foresail be boomed out to leeward, as this is against the rules. As the dinghy swings round to the new tack, there is a precise moment at which the sheet should be hauled, for if it is heaved in too soon, the sail will be backed—as in Figure 23—and the dinghy stopped; whilst if it is done too late it is harder to get it in properly and, of course, it will flap about uselessly in the meantime. The correct moment will soon be judged perfectly with a little practice.

When there is a sliding seat to deal with, as in *Hornets*, life is a little more complicated for the crew when changing tack, but with practice the management of the slide becomes almost second nature. If the crew is sitting out on the end of the slide, with his feet on the gunwale, he will have to come in when the helmsman begins to turn the boat. Come in while the boat is still heeling to leeward—if you wait too long the boat will heel towards you and you will be trying to clamber uphill instead of downhill. Keep tension on the jib sheet as you slide in, but free it as soon as the jib shakes and while clearing the sheet, use the other hand to shoot the slide across. Then grab the new working sheet, sit on the slide, haul the sheet and push yourself out to windward as the sails fill. When running, centralise the slide, otherwise it may hit the water in a heavy roll and make steering very difficult. If the wind suddenly lets up when you are on the end of the plank and the boat heels steeply towards you it is very difficult to get inboard—uphill. In this emergency, let your feet slip down off the gunwale and fall forward onto your tummy, grab the slide and flop aboard like a sea-lion.

The technique with trapezes—wires from the hounds, one on each side of the mast, supporting the crew by a belt round the hips, so that he can lean right out with his feet on the gunwale—is similar. There is usually a hook on the trapeze belt to engage with an eye in the end of the windward trapeze wire. The crew has to slip inboard and unhook himself immediately the helm is put down for the turn, otherwise he may still be hooked on after the boat has passed the eye of the wind—and will then be on the leeward, not the windward trapeze—definitely a mistake. Having unhooked from the trapeze, clear the old working sheet, haul in the new one and hook the belt into the new windward trapeze wire. The crew cannot get outboard quite so quickly as with a sliding seat, but with good trapeze gear and practice very quick tacks can be made, and by bending and straightening the legs when supported by the wire, the crew's position is much more readily adjusted in puffy winds. Sliding seats are probably easier to begin with.

CHAPTER VI

CREWING (4)—WEIGHT DISTRIBUTION, BALANCE AND KICKING STRAPS

Effects of heeling—Maintaining equilibrium—Sitting out—Fore and aft trim—Light weather—Functions of a centreboard—Leeway—Lateral resistance—Centre of effort—Balance—Weather helm—Centreboard off the wind—Light airs—Kicking straps

ONE of the main functions of the crew is to assist in keeping the dinghy upright. It is true to say that all racing dinghies will sail faster upright than they will heeled, and although it is commonly thought that this applies only to boats with a V-shaped section it does, in fact, apply almost as much to those with more rounded bottoms. A little thought on the subject must render it obvious that a dinghy sailing along on her ear presents an underwater shape which is very far from being as efficient as that designed for the boat when she is upright. The very fact that the dinghy will create more splash and spray when she is sailing along on her side indicates, not that she is going faster, as one might at first be deceived into thinking, but that her passage is disturbing the water to a greater extent; in addition to this, her sails and centreboard will be less efficient and she will make more leeway. Figure 24 will give some indication of the undesirable results of allowing the boat to heel.

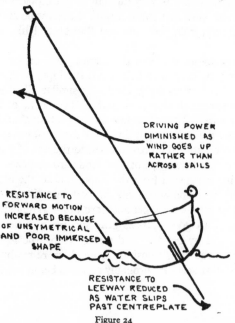

DRIVING POWER DIMINISHED AS WIND GOES UP RATHER THAN ACROSS SAILS

RESISTANCE TO FORWARD MOTION INCREASED BECAUSE OF UNSYMETRICAL AND POOR IMMERSED SHAPE

RESISTANCE TO LEEWAY REDUCED AS WATER SLIPS PAST CENTREPLATE

Figure 24

As already mentioned, the wind may be split from the sails to keep a dinghy upright; but the wind is the boat's propulsive force and to throw it away would be foolish when she may also be kept upright by the correct weight distribution of the human ballast aboard—when their avoirdupois fails, then must the wind be split, for it is even better to lose some driving power than to sail excessively heeled. Unfortunately it is not merely a question of sitting on the weather gunwale and staying there, because frequently the wind is varying considerably in strength, so that the crew must be very alert to throw his weight inboard or out to counteract and balance the whims of the wind. In a strong blow, when the maximum righting effect of the crew is needed, he should sit with the gunwale of the dinghy under his thighs, not (it is our misfortune) under the better padded parts of his anatomy, which should be well outboard. At least one foot should be tucked under the canvas toe strap provided on the centreboard case, but in uncertain and puffy winds it may be an advantage to keep the other foot in the bottom of the boat, to enable steadier and more controlled movements to be made. Figure 25 shows how the crew should place himself (it also applies to the helmsman) and the balance of forces which he is producing, whilst at the same time allowing the sails and the centreboard to act to the

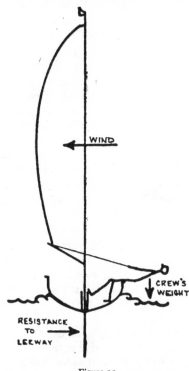

Figure 25

greatest advantage in producing headway and reducing leeway. The maximum righting effect of the crew is obtained when his weight is as far out as possible from the centre of buoyancy of the dinghy; in order to achieve this, the crew should keep his body horizontal—parallel to the surface of the water. It is a fallacy which has, most unfortunately, recently been given voice in the yachting press—that the crew should keep his body at right angles to the mast; the inaccuracy of this statement will be quickly realized after a glance at Figure 26. *The helmsman will also " sit the dinghy up," of course, but it should be the task of the crew to make the first move to counteract wind variations. As far as possible the crew and helmsman should endeavour to lean out to roughly the same degree and they should be

* CG in Figure 26 refers to the centre of gravity or weight of the crew.

fairly close together so as to reduce windage as much as they can, though it will be necessary for the skipper to lean out slightly less so that he may see past the crew.

The fore and aft trim of the dinghy is scarcely less important and the weight should be distributed so that, when going to windward, the

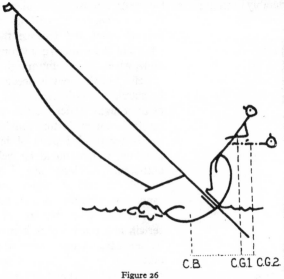

Figure 26

forefoot of the boat is immersed about an inch. Dinghies of different design vary as to the depth to which the forefoot should be immersed. The above is merely a general rule. The transom should then be just awash and not dragging in the water so as to cause suction aft. Off the wind, the weight should generally be moved aft a little, especially in stronger breezes, to counteract the depression of the bows due to the force of the wind pushing on the sails high above the centre of buoyancy.

In very light weather, so as to balance the weight of the skipper, who will probably wish to remain on the windward side in order to be able to see the sails properly, the crew will have to sit to leeward and, under these conditions, the boat should be heeled slightly to leeward. The underwater shape of the hull is of less importance at low speeds than the friction of the water on the immersed portions of the hull, which may be reduced in area by a slight heel, whilst at the same time the sails, which will not be filled by a very light wind into their most efficient curves, can be assisted by gravity to produce the desired flow by means of a slight cant. There is a tendency for crews to move aft slightly, when sitting inboard or to leeward, and this should be avoided. Unfortunately, it is not comfortable sitting to leeward in most dinghies, especially if the boat is off the wind and a certain amount of centreboard is up, but the crew should endeavour to keep still in light weather and, if possible, should keep his head away from the foresail where it might disturb the wind flow. When running, even in strong winds, the crew will almost certainly have to sit to leeward and a hand placed on the boom will do much towards steadying it and preventing it slatting about if there is a bit of a chop on the water.

The correct adjustment of the centreboard is scarcely less important than the proper trim of the sails. The function of the centreboard of a racing dinghy is primarily to prevent leeway, by providing lateral resistance. That is to say, their object is to prevent the boats from drifting sideways, (which reference to Figure 15 will show that they would otherwise do), by providing resistance to movement in that direction. If there is considerable weight in the centreboard, it will, of course, be a slight aid towards stability, but its righting effect does not come into operation with any great magnitude until the dinghy has already heeled much further than is good for her. A number of *International 14-footers* use very light wooden centreboards and the tendency in the *National 12's* is towards the lightest centreplates possible under the rules; this must surely confirm what those experienced in dinghy sailing realize, that the value of the centreboard as an aid to stability is extremely limited.

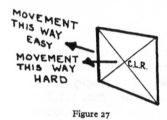

Figure 27

The term "lateral resistance" is one which will no doubt be readily understood and it is sufficient to point out that if a sheet of metal be drawn through the water edgeways on, there will be very little resistance to its passage, whereas, if one attempts to move it bodily sideways so that a flat surface is pressing on the water, there will be great resistance to its movement in that direction—lateral resistance, in fact. When the plate is at rest, the centre through which this force or resistance works can be geometrically found. In the case of the rectangular sheet shown in Figure 27, it is found by simply joining its opposite corners by two straight lines. The "centre of lateral resistance" is at the intersection of those two lines. This point on a dinghy can be found practically by an experiment, which, though simple enough in itself, has certain actual difficulties when performed, unless it is carried out on a perfectly windless day in still water. The method is as follows : the dinghy's centreplate is lowered and the rudder fixed by the tiller, lashed amidships. A rod is used to touch the gunwale about amidships and the boat pushed sideways, away from the experimenter, who stands abeam of the dinghy. If the rod is pushing the gunwale ahead of the centre of lateral resistance, as at A in Figure 28, the stern will swing towards him; but if the rod is pushing aft of the centre of lateral resistance, as at B in Figure 28, the bow will swing towards him; the whole boat will move bodily sideways if the rod is pushing directly above the centre of lateral resistance, as at C in the figure to which we are referring. In practice, the point will

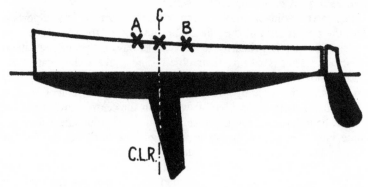

Figure 28

be found rather by trial and error—first the bows swinging towards the observer and then the stern, rather than the exact centre being determined by bodily sideways movement of the dinghy. The centre of lateral resistance is usually referred to by the letters C.L.R.

The " centre of effort " of the sails can also be found geometrically and this is the point through which the power of the wind on the sails is, theoretically, transmitted. We cannot go deeply into the matter here, but when the boat is designed it should be arranged that the centre of effort (C.E.) of the sails falls slightly *ahead* of the C.L.R. This is done because when the boat moves forward the C.L.R. moves towards the bow and, therefore, will come directly under the C.E. ; the dinghy will then be "balanced" and no pressure will be needed on the rudder to keep the boat on a straight course. Unfortunately, however, as the speed of the boat increases further, the C.L.R. will continue to move forward and the boat will again become unbalanced. Now it must be obvious that, when the rudder is moved to either side of the midline, there is a braking, as well as a turning, effect on the dinghy and it is therefore very desirable for the helm not to deviate from the centreline of the hull more than is essential for actual alterations in course. If the mainsail is sheeted in hard in a beam wind, the tendency will be for this sail to push the boat's stern to leeward and weather helm is produced. Racing model yachts are sometimes steered on a course by the relative trim of the mainsail and foresail producing a tendency to luff or bear away as the case may be.

Now the lateral resistance of the dinghy is afforded not only by the centreboard, but by the hull itself and, to a certain extent, the rudder ; but of these the centreboard is the most important and, luckily, being pivoted, can be moved forward and aft so as somewhat to counteract the movements of the two centres under discussion. As previously stated, a well-designed dinghy should be "balanced" when going to windward at slow to moderate speeds upright; but as the speed is increased and the C.L.R. moves further forward, she will become unbalanced—she will, in fact, carry "weather helm"; which means that, in order to keep the boat on a given straight course, the tiller will have to be moved towards the weather side of the dinghy. Figure 29 will make this clear. This state of affairs would be most annoying were it not for the fact that there is a cure, which lies in the correct manipulation of the centreboard; by altering the fore and aft position of this,

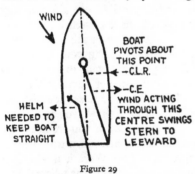

Figure 29

the C.L.R. can be kept more or less immediately below the C.E. and proper balance maintained at varying speeds. Thus, in strong winds when going to windward, the centreboard should usually be slightly raised (this of course also has the effect of swinging a pivoted centreboard aft). When reaching, the tendency towards weather helm is greater still and, as the inclination of the boat to slide to leeward is reduced on this point of sailing, the centreboard is not so necessary to prevent leeway and may therefore be hauled up still further, until it is about half way to being completely raised—perhaps more. On a dead run, the centreboard is performing no duties with regard to leeway and may be hauled up completely, thus further reducing any tendency towards weather helm and also the resistance due to skin friction and the passage of the centreboard through the water. In heavy weather, however, or in a loppy sea, the centreboard may sometimes be left partly down to reduce rolling, which may become extreme in dinghies before the wind, especially in the *National 12's*.

The helmsman is in a better position to judge when the dinghy is properly balanced than is the crew; and so the final adjustment of the centreboard is better decided by him. But it is the crew's job to make the rough adjustments which become desirable on alterations of course—from a beat to a reach, perhaps—and the skipper may then indicate the precise position later, when the opportunity presents itself.

In light weather it is very important that as few movements as possible be made and they should be steady, slow and catlike. Try to imagine a smooth stream of air over the sails and a regular flow of water past the hull (though of course it is the hull which moves—not the water), and then consider what happens when you suddenly wobble the sails, hull and centreboard from side to side. The steady passage of air and water is upset and eddies are created which hover around for a considerable time before everything settles down again and the two elements, which support and propel the boat, are smoothly moving over the surfaces with which they are in contact.

The importance of the crew keeping a good look-out has already been mentioned and should hardly need stressing. Apart from the disposition of rival competitors—especially those on a converging course—it is invaluable to the helmsman if the crew can give reliable information as to changes of direction of current, as indicated by the swing of moored vessels and so on, and, if possible, can also note any outstanding gain by other competitors who have chosen a course the virtues of which may have been doubtful to your own skipper. Avoid, at all costs, being pessimistic, or the risk of letting your helmsman imagine that you are "back-seat driving"—be certain that he knows that you are giving him information only and not advice. Turning marks at sea and some of them inland are often hard to see at a distance and the crew should make every effort to locate them as soon as possible and tell the skipper immediately he can see them. If you are not quite certain that it is the right mark, indicate to the helmsman that there is doubt in your mind, but nevertheless show him where it is—he may be able to decide if it is the right one. When showing the whereabouts of a mark to your skipper, it is as well not to point to it with outstretched arm, for remember that all your competitors will be also seeking out the mark and there is no good reason why you should present them all with gratuitous information, which may enable them to reach it before you do.

The kicking strap, or boom vang, is a vital part of the rigging of a racing dinghy; were it not so, it would most certainly have been discarded, because of the discomfort that it may cause the crew and the limitation of movement which it tends to impose upon him. The object of the kicking strap is to prevent the boom from rising excessively, when the mainsheet is eased off and therefore ceases to exert a downward pull on it. When the boom rises, the top part of the mainsail may blow well ahead of the mast and cease to draw effectively. If the situation goes one stage worse, the lower part of the sail may gybe across to the other side, leaving the top part on the same side as it was before, so that the sail is twisted, as in Figure 30. This is called a "Chinese gybe" and is very likely to cause a capsize, or to tear the sail on a spreader, and, in any case, it is far from easy to remedy once it has occurred. In spite of the fact that it may occasionally attempt to guillotine you, therefore, the kicking strap is an ally whose worth entitles it to proper use.

Usually, it will consist of a length of wire or rope, probably with a two-fold purchase for tautening it up, and rigged as described in

Chapter III; this arrangement allows the boom to swing quite freely to either side, of course, but at the same time keeps it down. On

International 14-footers and some other dinghies which reef fairly frequently, the upper end may be made fast to a clawring on the boom, which will permit the rotation of the boom for roller reefing whilst the kicking strap is still in position. Some boats will be found to have elastic kicking straps—though it is hard to see the reason why, for if they have sufficient tension on them to exert a great enough downward pull on the boom, they will be very hard to remove from the

Figure 30

latter when they are not needed. On the smaller dinghies especially, in which the space for the crew is very restricted when the kicking strap is in position, a quick method of releasing it from the boom should be provided; this may be arranged as in Figure 31. If this is the case, it is advisable to set the kicking strap to exactly the right tension before

a race in the following manner: get your helmsman to sail the dinghy with the mainsheet very slightly eased and sweat up hard on the kicking strap tackle. This will put sufficient tension on it to keep the boom at the right level and will mean that it will come slightly slack when the mainsail is close-hauled and the boom pulled down by the mainsheet; it will therefore be possible to remove the kicking

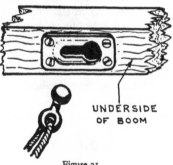

UNDERSIDE OF BOOM

Figure 31

strap from the boom without difficulty when tacking. If the kicking strap is removed in this way, never, on any account, forget to fit it again before the end of your tacking; it will be extremely hard to fix it and get the right tension on it once the dinghy is turned off the wind. Keep the kicking strap in place before the start, even if the first leg of the course is a tack—it can be removed after the starting gun has gone, if opportunity permits, but it may be useful during gybes occurring in last-minute manoeuvres when jockeying for starting positions.

CHAPTER VII

CREWING (5)—HEAVY AND LIGHT WEATHER TASKS

Heavy weather technique—Preventing a capsize—Running and gybing in a strong wind—Planing—Reefing—Righting a capsize—A swamped dinghy —Towing—Anchoring—Sum up

IN heavy weather, dinghy racing becomes really hard work and very exciting and exhilarating. The main point to remember is, of course, that the boat should be sailed as upright as possible all the time, both to windward and off the wind. The *National* 12's and *Fireflies* seldom reef, because it has been found that in these classes a reefed dinghy will seldom be able to keep up with one carrying full sail over a course on which there is sailing both on and off the wind. This means that frequently the boats may be rather heavily over-canvassed to windward, in order that they may have all the sail area they need to get maximum planing speed off the wind. Much of the wind has therefore to be spilt from the mainsail in the strongest puffs and the dinghy will at such times sail along with only her foresail pulling. Though this technique has perhaps to be applied more frequently to the dinghies in the two classes just mentioned, it also applies, to an only slightly smaller extent, to all the other racing dinghy classes. The importance of keeping the foresail properly full of wind under these conditions has been previously emphasized and it cannot be too strongly stressed.

If so strong a squall hits the boat that the skipper needs the foresail eased, as well as the mainsail, in order to prevent a capsize, let the sail right out so that it flaps freely and throw your weight to windward absolutely as far as you can to prevent the capsize. When the boat comes up again, she will probably have lost way and may be blown astern by the heavy wind; the sails may fill on either tack when she begins to sail again and you should not haul your foresail immediately she comes up, unless it is obvious that the sail will fill properly to leeward. Do not back your sail to pay the dinghy's head off to leeward unless the helmsman tells you to—he may be trying to get her to sail off in the other direction, if she has gathered sternway and, in any case, backing the foresail might cause a capsize if another squall hits the dinghy.

A *Firefly* in the Hamble River. The boom is held down by the
kicking strap and the mainsail sets perfectly

Planing in a *National 12*. Helmsman and crew lean aft. Helmsman hauls in the mainsheet to trim the mainsail to the new "apparent wind" direction. (Page 71)

When running before a strong wind, it is frequently advisable for the helmsman and crew to sit as far as possible towards the opposite sides of the dinghy in order to reduce, to some extent, the tendency towards rolling. When, however, a gybe has to be executed, they should both come to the middle of the boat as the helm is put over, so that they are both able to put their weight where it is wanted immediately after the sails have swung across. During a gybe the foresail may get somewhat wrapped up round the forestay, but a good pull on the sheet will clear it. The centreboard should be lowered at least half way before a heavy-weather gybe is attempted, to reduce any rolling that may take place as a result of it.

Nearly all the dinghies in the classes which have been mentioned in this book will plane when on a reach in a strong or moderately strong wind. That is to say that the boat will actually be lifted up by the force of her forward motion on the water and will skim over it at a speed far in excess of her previous rate. In some dinghies this happens quite suddenly and the change from ordinary sailing to planing is dramatic and sharp; in other cases—*Merlin-Rockets* especially—there is a steady increase in speed and the conversion from the usual displacement sailing into planing is not so marked.

In some boats, just before planing speed is reached, the bows may seem to be actually depressed (this is particularly the case in some of the smaller dinghies), and the dinghy may seem to be threatened with swamping from her own bow wave. At this stage, a united heave outboard and aft on the part of the helmsman and crew will probably jerk the dinghy up on to her own bow wave, as it were, and she will then get the wave under her shoulders, instead of around them, and will tear away like a scalded cat. Directly she begins to plane, the apparent wind to which we referred in Chapter V, will come ahead slightly, because of the increased speed (the length of AC, in Figure 18, is increased), and so the sails must be sheeted-in somewhat. At the same time, the tendency of the dinghy to heel is reduced and the crew will probably have to shift his weight inboard. In many cases the weight has to be moved aft considerably before the boat can be got to plane properly, but this is not always so. It is easy to tell when a dinghy is planing, because her wake flattens out a long way astern of her, whilst the bow wave comes well aft and she may feel as though she is flying over, rather than through, the water. When she is travelling like this, do not jiggle about in the boat or you may knock her off her perch. Sit still, hold your hat on, and let it happen.

Reducing sail when under way is not a very easy operation but has only to be done occasionally. Shaking out a reef is more frequently necessary, for races are usually started to windward, if possible, when reduced sail in a strong blow is an advantage until the dinghy has reached the weather mark and is no longer going to windward ; the reef will then often be shaken out to increase speed off the wind, even if it means having to sail with too much canvas on the next windward leg ; it will nearly always be done on the last leg of a race, if there is no more windward work.

Most racing dinghies reef their mainsails by rotating the boom and therefore rolling the sail up around it. *Cadets* are an exception to this rule and their mainsails are reefed by tying cords or reef points, which are sewn through the sail about a quarter of the way up from the boom, around the bolt rope, the sail being folded neatly along the boom and reef knots being used on the reef points. Tie down the luff reef cringle first, then pull the sail out fairly taut along the boom and secure the leech cringle ; the reef cringles are eyes sewn into the luff and leech of the sail. Next secure the reef points, starting with those at either end and working towards the middle of the sail. On no account should the reef points be tied under the boom, as this may pull the sail out of shape and, at best, will make an untidy job of it. Reefing or unreefing should not be attempted when under way with the sails up in these little boats.

On some dinghies in which winches are permitted, there is one on the mast, the operation of which pulls on a wire rope which rotates the boom and rolls up the sail. To unreef when under way, the boom is allowed to rotate, thus releasing the sail, which is hoisted up by the main halliard winch at the same time, if possible— tension being kept on the luff of the sail all the time to reduce the strains on the mast groove in which the bolt rope runs. Many *National* 12's and *Merlin-Rockets* have shouldered pins to the gooseneck, which fit into square holes in the end of the boom ; the boom is rotated by hand, when the sail is reefed, and then pushed on to the pin which prevents it unwinding. This is very neat, but imposes rather a strain on the gooseneck. The strain, may, nevertheless, be much reduced if the gooseneck slides in a length of track secured to the mast, as in Figure 32. When unreefing with such an arrangement, the downhaul should first be released and the sail hauled as high as possible by the main halliard ; the boom is then pushed

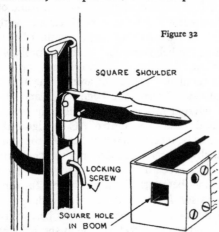

Figure 32

SQUARE SHOULDER

LOCKING SCREW

SQUARE HOLE IN BOOM

aft a little, to permit its rotation, and the sail will then unroll—the boom becoming lower and the gooseneck sliding down the track as this takes place ; the sail may then be hauled up, if necessary, by the halliard and the luff tensioned by downhauling the gooseneck. The kicking strap will, of course, require consequential adjustment. Off the wind, it will not be found an easy matter either to hoist or lower the mainsail, as it will be pressing on the shrouds and spreaders, and care must be taken to ensure that it does not get torn. When reefing, the above operations are reversed.

Another job associated with heavy weather is bailing. There is not much to be said about this, except that care should be taken not to do too much damage to the dinghy with the bailer whilst you are trying to clear the boat of water. It is a waste of time to try and get the bailer completely full every time you lift it up, because probably half of it will spill before you manage to get it over the side. If the boat gets very full, as a result of a partial capsize or something, do not bother to try and fill the bailer at all, but endeavour to scoop or "hoosh" the water over the side in one motion. Most bailing operations will be carried out when sailing off the wind and, if it is merely a question of getting a couple of bucketsful of spray out of the dinghy, a big sponge is by far the best thing to do it with ; it can be squeezed out with one hand, by pressing it against the foredeck (ahead of the coaming, please), or outside of the hull. The removal of water from a racing dinghy is not done for the comfort of those aboard, but for the sake of the sailing qualities of the hull ; two bucketsful of water emptied into the bottom of a dinghy looks very little, but it weighs over forty pounds and it is not much use for the owner to drill little holes in his fittings and so on, in his anxiety to make them a few ounces lighter, if the dinghy is allowed to sail about with forty pounds of useless weight slopping around the leeward bilge. Pumps are permitted in *Merlin-Rockets*, but not in the others; they are to be recommended in some of the boats in this class, because of the difficulty of passing a bailer of water through the narrow space between the deck and the centreboard case.

Capsizing is a misfortune which occasionally occurs even to the best dinghy sailor. In the case of some *Merlin-Rockets* and *Cadets*, with wide decks specially designed to keep the boat from filling up when capsized, it should be possible to get the dinghy upright and sailing again in a very short time, simply by easing the sheets completely and levering her up, with a foot on the keel or centreboard and hands on the gunwale, as in Figure 33. If a good stopper-knot was put in the foresheet when the boat was rigged, the sheet may be used to haul on, as shown in Figure 34. It will be far harder to get her upright if the sails have been allowed to get in the water, but, if you are quick, this should never happen. Climb back aboard as she rights ; it is unnecessary, in fact foolish, to bounce on the centreboard in an effort to heave her up—if she won't right with the application of your weight in the proper place, all the bouncing in the world will make no difference, except, possibly, to break or bend the centreboard.

Dinghies in other classes will fill with water when capsized, but will, of course, float more or less high because of their buoyancy apparatus.

Figure 33

From this point of view, modern *National* 12's will probably be found best, for it is possible to sail some of them even when filled to capacity with water and, in these boats, the water can be bailed out and the dinghy sail on. With other dinghies a capsize usually means

having to give up the race, although, if the boat can be righted and bailed out without any assistance, this is perfectly legal and the race may be continued; but no outside help at all may be accepted, either in getting the boat ashore or in getting her empty.

Dinghies with only a little buoy-ancy in excess of the minimum laid down in the class rules will be unstable after being righted in a waterlogged condition, but, with the helmsman on one side and the

Figure 34

crew on the other, it should be possible to hold her level and bail some of the water out whilst swimming alongside. Directly sufficient water is out, one of the crew may get aboard and continue bailing—scooping the water out, as mentioned earlier—and eventually the other may climb in and the dinghy be finally cleared of water whilst sailing. This is impossible in a choppy sea, when the waves will slop in over the gunwale as quickly as the crew can bail it out; it is also impossible in dinghies which are not fitted with rubber across the centreboard slot in the keel.

If you do not intend to try and finish the race and a tow is to be accepted, the first thing to do is to lower the sails. This may not be easy in the case of the mainsail, as the bolt rope will shrink immediately it gets wet and it may not be possible to uncleat the halliard, if winches are not used; in this case, the halliard will have to be unshackled from the head of the sail while the boat is on her side and the masthead at water level. It is not always easy to find, fit and operate the winch handle, when both it and the winch are submerged. The boat can subsequently be righted and cleared of water, as previously explained. When making the towline fast, do so round a thwart—and not the forestay or mast. The towrope should be stopped to the forestay, to prevent the dinghy sheering under tow and the foresheets or any other handy line may be used for this. She will tow better if the weight of the crew is well aft and the rudder, kept amidships, will act as a skeg and steady her. As soon as a dinghy which has been capsized in salt water is brought ashore, the inside of her mast should be hosed out with fresh water to remove the salt. The inside of hollow wooden masts is not varnished and, if saturated with salt, the wood will nearly always be damp and will, in time, deteriorate.

Anchoring is permitted during a race and in very light weather, when there are adverse currents, the kedge is frequently used. Make certain that the line is not fouling the anchor before you drop it. As a rule it is best to put it over to windward just by the main shrouds, or further forward, if you can get it there, but of course you are not allowed to hurl it forward. Let out the line fast until the anchor reaches the bottom and then more slowly until it holds and the dinghy ceases to move astern. If there is a strong current, directly the anchor is holding, the water will rush past the boat, which will appear to be moving forward at quite a pace ; steerage way, which may previously have been almost lost, will be considerable and the helmsman should be told how the cable is lying, so that he does not allow the dinghy to get over it and get it caught on the centreplate. If a cable drum or reel is used for the line, it may be a good plan to put this on your arm when letting the line out, so that the reel rotates on the limb as though the latter were its axle. When getting the anchor in, haul the line as fast as you can if the dinghy is sailing forward over it ; but if the anchor is still ahead, haul it in slowly at first, but ever faster, so that you do not break it out at your first pull, but haul the dinghy forward a little at a gradually accelerated speed until the anchor breaks out as the line comes almost vertical. Do not bother to roll it up on its drum as you get it in—there is not time for this—but it should be done later if you get an opportunity. The anchor must always be recovered after use, or the dinghy is disqualified under the rules of the R.Y.A.

It will be unnecessary to mention that concentration on the job is essential in a good crew—so is obedience to a helmsman's orders, for if there is any argument amongst the team that sails the boat, chaos and inefficiency must result. An order from the helmsman should be treated as a command, to be carried out immediately—not a signal for a debate. Perhaps the most important attribute that a crew can possess is the will to win.

There is a lot for a good crew to do and some helmsmen may seem to demand almost the impossible, but the reward is great and the thrill of a well-sailed race is an experience which gives an immense and lasting feeling of satisfaction.

CHAPTER VIII

HELMING (1)—HELMSMAN'S RESPONSIBILITIES

Understanding of crew's tasks—Explaining aims—Fitting centreboards—
Stepping masts—Tensioning sails—Useful and essential gear—Studying
the course—Leaving and approaching the shore

THE chapters which precede this one are scarcely less relevant to the helmsman than is this and they should not be overlooked by him. Perhaps you may have heard of the two bargemen endeavouring to execute some difficult manoeuvre which is still not accomplished after several attempts involving much hard work on the foredeck by the mate; eventually sweating and exasperated, the latter straightens his back and calls aft to the skipper, "You can do what you like with your perishin' end; my end's made fast." Well, this kind of thing can't go on in a dinghy, any more than it can in a barge. Both ends are joined together pretty firmly and what is done at one end affects the other. It is inevitable, therefore, that there is a lot of overlapping of jobs and a helmsman can never be really first class unless he completely understands the crew's tasks and the difficulties that may be encountered in doing them.

In the crew's chapter on sailing we emphasized the importance of trying to understand the skipper, of making allowances for the possibility of overwrought nerves relieving themselves by verbal chastisement of the crew, slander of the other competitors and unparliamentary abuse of the weather, the course and everything else within sight. Many people are helped by such outbursts, when inwardly they are cursing themselves for having made a bad start. But if only a helmsman can be bold enough to say to his crew, "I'm afraid we've made a rotten start; so now we must work like blazes to make up for it," there is no doubt that he will get more efficiency and co-operation from the other end of the dinghy. A skipper who keeps nagging at his crew lays himself wide open to the latter's criticism, which would doubtless be taken most unkindly, for it is unlikely that the skipper himself is sailing a perfect race.

As helmsman, you should try to take your crew into your confidence and explain to him, as far as possible, what you are aiming at, both when rigging the boat and when sailing (Figure 35). In this way you will get more intelligent co-operation and foresight from your crew than could be expected from one kept in ignorance of his skipper's aims. If things go wrong and your tactics in a race do not produce the results you hoped for, it is unlikely that your foresheet hand will lose confidence in you; for he will realize that at least you knew what you were trying to do and that there are often cases where chances must be

taken, and little blame will be due if they do not meet with success every time. Furthermore, in this way, you will be doing a valuable job in maintaining his interest and helping him to make a really good crew, who may one day assist his country to gain and maintain a high position in international sailing matches. In addition, such explanations will assist you to

Figure 35

make the correct decisions, for it is unlikely that you will lay your plans bare to the criticism—even though it be unspoken—of your crew, without first giving them very careful consideration. It is not suggested that you should give a running commentary during the race, for there is no opportunity for this, nor that you explain anything much besides the proper rigging of the boat, the correction of crewing faults and your reasons for carrying out the racing tactics which you choose. Experienced crews will, of course, know almost as well as you what you are trying to do.

Most of the tasks which have to be done when rigging a dinghy are explained in Chapter III and it is only necessary to mention here some of the jobs that are generally dealt with exclusively by the skipper.

Centreboards are usually removed when the dinghy is stored for a long time or sometimes when trailing from one place to another and, in order to replace them, it is generally necessary to roll the dinghy on to one side, taking care to see that there are plenty of soft things under her bilge, for the protection of her planking, before doing so. The

point of balance of most dinghies, when they are on their sides, will usually be when they are beyond the vertical, as shown in Figure 36, and they can quite easily be held in this position by one person whilst the other inserts the upper end of the centreboard into the slot in the keel, taking care to see that the

Figure 36

leading edge is facing forward. The board should be pushed towards the bows until the leading edge comes into contact with the bolt on which it is suspended and pivots; it should then be pushed further into the slot, the leading edge being kept in contact with the bolt, until the latter slips into the slit in the board; the board may then be pulled back a little to ensure that it is correctly positioned and then pivoted aft, on its bolt, into the box. The hoisting tackle is then made fast and cleated, and the boat lowered back on to an even keel.

The handling and stepping of masts is something which calls for knack rather than strength or skill. Different masts, naturally, require different handling, and it is impossible to deal with each type in detail here. Let us first consider one of the most simple masts to put up—

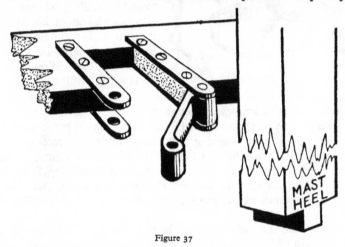

Figure 37

that of a *National 12-footer* which is stepped on the keel, with a gate in the mast thwart to hold it there, as shown in Figure 37. The weight of such a mast, complete with all its rigging, will be about 17 pounds and its centre of gravity will be about three-eighths of the way from the foot or heel of the spar—about 9 feet in this case—(in some classes, this point has to be marked and so is easily found and should be remembered). In *Swordfish* and some *Merlin-Rockets* it will generally be relatively nearer to the heel, whilst in *Fireflies* it will be rather further from the heel. Obviously, when carrying the mast, it is better to do so at this point. Before putting it upright, make certain that you have removed all the twine stoppings with which you may have secured the stays and halliards to the mast. When getting it upright, hold it with one hand just below the point of balance and with the other about 2½ feet towards the heel; lift it up above your head and pull downwards with the hand nearer to the heel; as the mast nears the vertical, slide the upper hand down a little and rest the heel on the ground. Figure 38 will assist in showing the correct method of carrying and erecting the mast. If you have to carry it in a vertical position, do so with your hands

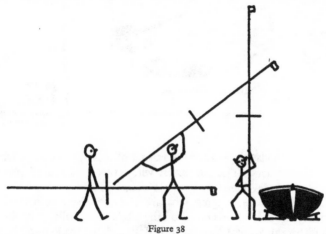

Figure 38

fairly well separated so that you have more control over it and can easily keep it upright. Having opened the gate in the mast thwart, you may now lift the mast over the gunwale of the dinghy and into position. Grip the mast with your hands well spaced, as before, but with the upper hand about level with your chin and bend your knees so that, when you straighten up and lift, the heel of the mast will clear the gunwale. As soon as the mast is inside the dinghy, tilt it aft somewhat and insert the heel into its slot in the keel, after which the spar may be tilted carefully forward so that it enters the space provided for it in the mast thwart and it can be secured by the mast gate. When the mast is in, the forestay and shrouds should be attached as soon as possible; until these are fixed, the mast is extremely delicate and might even be broken, where it is crossed by the thwart, by the force of a strong gust of wind on the upper part. Take great care not to jerk the rigging, when fixing it, or this too may damage the mast.

If the mast is stepped on deck in some form of "inkpot" stepping, as many are (see Figure 39), the dinghy may be unchocked on one side and allowed to lie on her keel and bilge keel at an angle in order to facilitate the fitting of the mast. The forestay and the higher shroud may then be attached to their appropriate positions on the dinghy and the mast lifted upright, slipped into its stepping and allowed to heel over in keeping with the angle of the dinghy, when it will be supported to some extent by the forestay and shroud already made fast; the other shroud can then be grasped and attached. As a precaution, the crew can hold on to the unattached shroud as the mast is being lifted up;

Figure 40 shows this being done. Many deck-stepped masts are erected without the boat being heeled and, as already stated, there are many

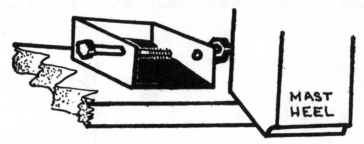

MAST
HEEL

Figure 39

different methods adopted for the raising of masts, some of which are better than others. The two given will act as guides until personal techniques are developed.

Most of the other rigging jobs are given in the crew's chapters, except for the correct tensioning on the edges of the sails. The foresail is simple in this respect, because it is designed and made to be hoisted as taut as possible by the halliard; for this reason a wire rope is sewn into the luff of this sail, to withstand the pull. In some cases, the foresail luff may also be made to act as the forward support of the mast, the forestay itself being of very light wire and becoming quite slack when the foresail halliard is sweated up tight (see Figure 5).

Generally speaking, it is desirable to put rather more tension on the luff and foot of the mainsail in heavy weather, than on light days. The reason for this is that the tension on the bolt ropes should be such that they are stretched to the same degree as the canvas of the sails, and so do not pucker the sails by being insufficiently taut nor stretch them by being too taut; in heavy weather, the sailcloth will be stretched by the force of the wind to a greater extent than it would be in less of a blow. In addition to this, the well-tensioned bolt ropes will tend to flatten the sail a little and will counteract to some extent the tendency of the strong wind to produce too much flow in the sail. With a new sail, very great care must be taken over its original stretching; it should never be used for the first time on a wet or windy

Figure 40

day, but should be gradually stretched on a calm, sunny day, when the dinghy should be sailed gently with eased sheets for a couple of hours, while the slack is gradually taken up in the bolt ropes. It will be noticed that the cloth of a new sail is wrinkled near the bolt ropes; this is because the rope will stretch more than the canvas and so the sailmaker leaves the latter a little slack, as this will be taken up as the rope stretches. The luff of a new dinghy sail may stretch as much as 12 inches and, until it is stretched, the boom may droop at its outer end considerably.

Leech lines are usually sewn in the after edges of mainsails and sometimes foresails, but as a general rule they are best left quite slack, and care should be taken to see that there is plenty of loose line left free whilst the sail is stretching.

Figure 41

A few items of equipment that are valuable or essential in a racing dinghy but which are not usually provided by the builder, may be mentioned here. The first necessity is a good racing flag. An excellent one may be made out of aluminium tubing for the mast and brass wire for the frame, as shown in Figure 41. Such a flag will react to the merest breath of air, and the counterbalance weight, which can be made of copper or lead wire wrapped round and round the brass wire support and then covered with putty to smooth it off, should be arranged so that it is just not sufficiently heavy to balance the weight of the frame and the material of the flag; if it is arranged thus, it will not spin round so much when you are sailing in light weather in a bit of a lop, but will lie far more still and steady. The frame should not entirely surround the fabric, as this would make a very rigid affair; it is harder to place faith in a contraption which gives no indication at all that it is being affected by the wind—a slight flutter in the lower part of the flag increases one's faith in it as a wind indicator and, to a limited extent, gives some idea of the wind strength as well as direction.

Another useful, but not essential, piece of equipment, is a reel on which to wind the anchor cable when not in use. These used to be obtainable from shops selling electric flex and cable. The reel should be given a good coat of paint, especially on the edges of the sides of the drum, which are generally made of plywood of the non-waterproof variety.

In classes which do not use spinnakers, a jib-stick, with which to boom out the foresail on the opposite side to the mainsail when on a run, is quite essential. This should be as light as possible and should float, in case it is dropped overboard. The method of attaching it to the mast and the sail should be as foolproof as possible and not fiddlesome or difficult to work with wet and cold fingers. The method devised by the writer for his dinghy appears to be amongst the best and is shown in Figure 42 ; the cup on the jib-stick is simply pushed on to the ball-fitting on the mast—the sides of the cup springing slightly open to

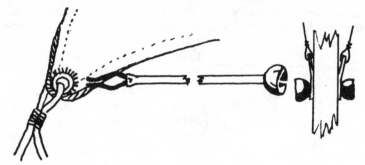

Figure 42

allow this and then grasping the mast fitting tightly enough to hold the stick in place, though allowing it to move freely in all directions ; the outer end is merely pushed into the clew eye of the foresail and stays there, because of the spring action of the wire prong.

A net, bag or some other means of stowing the spinnaker, if carried, should most certainly be provided in order to keep the sail safe and clear of any water that may be in the bottom of the boat.

The remainder of the jobs associated with rigging the boat are given in the crew's chapters, as it is desirable that he should understand how to do them all ; but, of course, many of these tasks will be carried out by the skipper, and he should, most certainly, check the gear in his boat himself carefully before going afloat.

If you are racing, you should make quite certain of the course and it is usually well worth while taking the trouble to prepare a small sketch map if it is at all complicated. If the race is an important one to you and the marks are likely to be difficult to discern, such a chartlet will be quite invaluable to you during the race, especially if you have previously been able to note any easily recognized objects ashore or on the water, which may assist you in finding the less conspicuous mark around which you are to sail. These chartlets, which may also have a little tidal information on them, can be rendered less vulnerable to wet by a coat of shellac varnish, which dries in a few minutes, or even by rubbing them over with floor polish.

You should also familiarize yourself with the time of the start and the class flag and other signals or flags which may apply to your race. Your stop watch, or other timing watch, should be wound and allowed to run a little while before you go afloat, so that you may be certain that it is in proper working order, but remember to return stop watches to zero after stopping them.

When your dinghy has been launched, it is generally best to let the crew get aboard first and a little centreboard may usually be lowered. If she is in deep enough water to permit the fitting of the rudder and tiller, get your crew to do this, but make sure that he fits the pin to keep the tiller into the rudder head. The rudder will have to be fitted when under way, if the water is too shallow for it to be done before you get aboard. This is apt to be rather a tricky business and you may have to hold the rudder rather like a paddle in order to use it to steer until you are clear of obstructions and can get it on its hangings and fit the tiller and retaining pin. If your dinghy has a deck aft, the fitting of the rudder may be very awkward; it is best to lie flat on the deck, rather than attempt to kneel on it, because not only will the boat be more

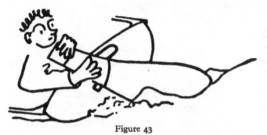

Figure 43

unstable with you in a kneeling position, but you may strain the deck, which is probably not designed to withstand much weight, by imposing a heavy local pressure on it, instead of somewhat spreading the load. Figure 43 shows how a rudder may be held like a paddle and used to steer the dinghy when in shallow water.

As soon as you have fitted the rudder and had the centreboard lowered, sail well out of the way of any other dinghies that may be leaving the shore, so as to give them plenty of room whilst their powers of manoeuvre are restricted.

Coming in to a weather shore is not difficult under most conditions; but when there is a swift current along the shore and a strong offshore wind, it may be advisable to get the foresail down before coming in, as the current will swing the dinghy's stern downstream directly her bow is held to the shore and the sails may then fill, whilst the foresail, if it is still set, may tend to pull her head off and make her difficult to manage. Generally speaking, however, it will be possible to bring the dinghy in under full sail. The retaining pin for the tiller should be removed well in advance and the tiller loosened somewhat in the rudder head. The crew can then be told to let the foresail sheets fly and to haul up the centreboard as the dinghy sails into shallow water. The speed of the boat can be controlled precisely by altering the trim of the mainsail and the sheet may be eased completely for the last twenty yards of the run in, whilst the tiller is removed and the rudder lifted off its hangings shortly before it would strike the bottom. If there is anything more than a very light air, it is best to lower the sails whilst the crew stands in shallow water holding the dinghy head to wind, but if there are plenty of hands to help you lift her ashore it may be done with the sails still up.

When coming in to a lee shore, with the wind aft, it is essential to lower the mainsail some distance from the shore in winds that are anything more than a feeble breath. As this job mainly falls to the lot of the crew, it is largely dealt with in Chapter IV and it is only necessary to say here that the dinghy must, of course, be turned head to wind before the sail is lowered; it will be found that her bows blow off to leeward again as soon as the main is down. If the wind is very strong, it may be wise to lower the foresail also, before the shore is reached, and carry on in at the speed produced by the windage on the mast and hull. It may also be wise to lower the mainsail, even when landing on a weather shore, if the race has finished a long way from where you have to beach your boat and it is blowing very strongly. After a gruelling race, one tends to be rather less alert and the reaction after crossing the finishing line is, frequently, to become careless—it is so annoying to capsize after the race is over when there is no need to have a lot of canvas set and it is far better to get the bulk of it down and take things more easily. Nearly all racing dinghies will sail to windward under the foresail only, but you should make certain that yours is capable of this before trying it, and do not attempt to sail quite so close to the wind as you would normally, for you will certainly be disappointed.

Though a few racing dinghies are kept on moorings, the majority of dinghy sailors will only seldom have to pick up a buoy. However, sooner or later nearly every racing helmsman will want to use a mooring, even if only temporarily, and should know how to put his boat on to it. Common sense and keen observation are the surest guides to the correct procedure and there are so many varying conditions of wind and current under which a mooring may have to be picked up that it is not intended here more than briefly to outline the more general principles involved. On currentless water, or with the wind blowing with the current, the operation is very simple, for the mooring is approached with the dinghy close-hauled and she is luffed-up towards the buoy with just sufficient way on her to take her up to it and bring it alongside by her main shrouds. Good judgement is needed to estimate the strength of the current and the amount of way that the dinghy will carry after luffing; charging on to a buoy is to be avoided, whilst it is highly annoying just to fail to reach it because you have luffed too soon. It is usually advisable to lower the foresail before approaching the mooring.

If the wind is blowing against a fairly strong current, the buoy will have to be approached downwind—against the current. The dinghy should be sailed a little up-wind of the mooring, luffed and stripped of her mainsail—meanwhile the current will be pushing her a little further up-wind. She can then bear away and sail for the buoy under her foresail on a broad reach or run, the sheet being eased and let fly to check her speed as the buoy is neared. Remember that a light shallow hull with a tall rig, such as that of a racing dinghy, is influenced greatly by the wind and proportionately less by the current; she may therefore lie up-tide of the buoy if the wind is very strong. Other moored craft may tell you how you may expect her to lie, but bear in mind the characteristics of your own particular type of craft and do not take it for granted that she will swing in the same direction as a stocky cruising yacht.

Occasionally it happens that a dinghy has to lie to a buoy in an emergency—in a very heavy squall or because of broken gear. Sometimes the buoy may be far too big for her and the back-wash and eddy of the current down-tide of such a large object may continuously threaten to pull the boat violently towards the buoy and may cause serious damage. In such circumstances, pay out plenty of mooring line and stream a small bucket, if you have one, from the stern on the mainsheet. The resistance of this will pull the dinghy well back from the buoy. It should be pointed out that the resistance of a bucket streamed in this manner is very considerable and care should be exercised when using this method in a strong current, for otherwise the mooring line may be broken or other damage done. If you have no bucket, which is perhaps rather probable, the tiller, with a line made fast at either end so that it floats at right angles to the stream, may also do the trick. A bailer, tied by its handle to a line, might also work, but I have never tried this and it might swing about rather wildly in the current and become a nuisance.

CHAPTER IX

HELMING (2)—SAIL TRIMMING AND STEERING

Trim to windward—Off the wind—Kicking straps again—Holding the tiller extension and mainsheet—Changing tack—Spilling wind—Considerations of planing—Playing the mainsail—Meeting windshifts—Preventing a capsize to windward—Steering to windward—Tiller waggling—Feeling the helm—Producing balance—Planing and running in heavy weather

MUCH of what was said in Chapter III on the correct trimming of the foresail by the crew also applies to the handling of the mainsail by the skipper. The point at which the sail ceases to work efficiently may not be quite so obvious in the case of the mainsail as in that of the foresail, but it is usually indicated either by the trembling or fluttering of the leech of the sail or by the "lifting" of the luff—the appearance of which was described in Chapter V. A lifting luff may, however, be caused by a foresail sheeted in too hard and back-winding the main. If the headboard of the sail is very nearly in line with the racing flag or burgee—slightly inside, if anything— you won't be far wrong. As with the foresail, the mainsail will not draw very well if sheeted in hard and flat in very light winds and it should be eased a little under these conditions, so as to put more flow into the sail, and the dinghy sailed a trifle freer than normally.

When the dinghy is turned off the wind, the sheets are, of course, eased in accordance with the flag as a guide to correct trim. When the wind comes aft of abeam, or over the quarter or stern of the dinghy, the mainsail should be eased off so that the boom is up against the main shrouds. If, for any reason, a kicking strap is not used, the sheets should be eased rather less than they would be if the flow and twist in the sail was checked by a downward pull on the boom, otherwise drive will be lost in the upper part of the sail. In any case, when sailing without a kicking strap, your sail will be trimmed correctly only round about its middle third, because the third above it will be falling off too far to leeward and the lower third will have to be hauled up too far to windward to enable it to draw as it should, whilst, in addition to this, the sail will be pressed hard against the shrouds and rigging and be full of great creases and girts. Furthermore, the depressing effect on the bow will be far greater and you may suffer the indignity of seeing other dinghies plane past you, whilst their rude crews hold up ropes' ends

A planing *Swordfish*. The wake is flattened out and follows in
a continuation of the keel line of the after part of the hull—
a characteristic of the wave formation of a planing boat

An *International 14-footer* at Bourne End, on the Thames

to offer a tow and your boat wallows along in a welter of fussy froth. Figure 44 tells the story.

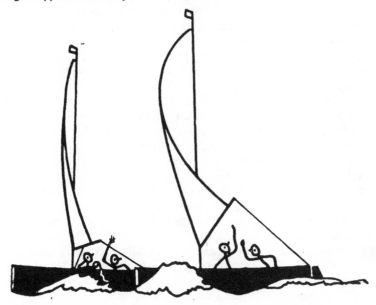

Figure 44

In nearly all modern racing dinghies, the mainsheet will be led from a horse or blocks on the transom to the hand. An extension will be provided on the tiller, so that you may steer comfortably whilst sitting the boat up, and it is surprising how quickly one gets accustomed to using these extensions, even though they may seem to be rather clumsy at first. If, for example, you are on the port tack and therefore sitting on the port gunwale in a moderate wind, or on the side bench in light airs, you will hold the tiller extension or tiller with your right hand and the mainsheet will come across your body and be held in the left hand. With the sheet coming across the body in this way, much of the strain is taken off your arms in heavy weather, as the elbow may be tucked well into the side and the forearm lie across the hip and so be supported by it, whilst the pull of the sheet is mostly taken on the body. The photograph on page 35, of a dinghy on a reach in a very gentle breeze, when the helmsman is sitting inside the boat and not using the tiller extension, shows how the mainsheet crosses the hand which holds the tiller. When the sheet has to be hauled, the hand on the tiller will grasp the rope, when the other has heaved in as much of it as it can in one pull, whilst the latter hand then catches hold of the sheet again near the tiller-hand and takes another heave.

If you are turning from port on to starboard tack, the procedure will be as follows : With your right hand, push the helm away from you deliberately, but not jerkily, at the same time easing the sheet a very little with your left hand (this is to allow the mainsheet block to slip across the horse from one side to the other quite easily). The dinghy will be turning quickly and your left leg should be put over the centre board case, whilst your right remains on the port side and you are then facing the stern in a somewhat crouching position (so as to lower your centre of gravity, thus reducing windage. Moreover, a boom may feel very hard when it smacks you smartly on the ear). The left knee may be placed against the tiller to keep it over to starboard while the sheet is changed from the left to the right hand, the left hand then being used to pivot the tiller extension round towards the stern and on to the starboard side. When the mainsheet block rattles across smartly to the other side of the horse, bring your right leg over the centreboard case, centralize the helm, sit on the gunwale and haul the sheet a little to the correct trim. Always look aloft at the flag to correct your course or the trim of the sails to the wind, directly after tacking. The whole procedure comes quite naturally and automatically after a very short time and, as has been stressed so often previously, you may well develop an individual technique which suits you better than that indicated here, which is intended solely as a reliable guide.

In strong gusts, there are two ways of preventing the dinghy from heeling excessively, apart from sitting out, which is naturally done as a

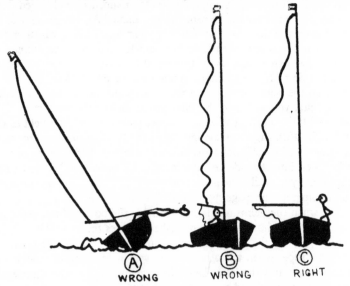

Figure 45

matter of course. The first method is to luff the boat's bow towards the wind (as at B, Figure 45), and the second is to keep the boat on her course, but ease the sheets somewhat, so that the sails are not at an angle to the wind which is "spilt" off them (as at C, Figure 45)— usually, it is only the mainsail that is eased in this way, except when it is necessary to relieve the sails of all wind pressure so as to prevent a capsize. The luffing method is not used when racing dinghies and is, in fact, never to be recommended for small boats except as a last resort to prevent a capsize, because the speed of the boat is drastically reduced and steerage way may be lost altogether. When this happens there is no stream of water going past the rudder which may be used to turn the boat, with the result that she is left unmanoeuvrable and at the mercy of a further gust which might come along and hit her from another angle. The dinghy should be maintained in an upright state, therefore, by the proper control of the sails and, because racing dinghies have their sail area split up between two sails, the wind may be spilt from one of these whilst the other still draws and pulls the boat along. Furthermore, on easing the sheet of a bermudian mainsail, such as is used in racing dinghies, the wind is first spilt from the upper part of the sail and from the rest of it on the further easing of the sheet; it is therefore possible to control, to a large extent, exactly how much wind is being allowed to press on the sails and, by letting the mainsheet fly out in a very heavy and vicious puff, we release a safety valve the effect of which is immediate.

Many of the established rules of seamanship are broken in dinghy racing; one is that a sailing boat should be reefed to suit the gusts, even if she is under-canvassed in the lulls. Such a practice could not be carried out with success in a dinghy race, in which precisely the opposite method is adopted, the dinghy being reefed to the lulls and relying on her helmsman to relieve her of excessive wind pressure in the gusts, by easing the mainsail or, if necessary, both sails. Dinghies such as *National 12's*, which do not carry additional sails, such as spinnakers, off the wind, seldom reef at all, because with modern planing hulls, maximum speed off the wind is limited almost solely by the amount of wind pressure pushing the boat along—so long as her gear can stand it— and not by the length of the hull or similar factors which play their part in displacement sailing. A planing hull has, in effect, no length, and therefore no theoretical maximum speed; whereas a displacement hull (one which is definitely displacing its own weight of water and not just skimming over it) has a theoretical maximum speed, depending on its length, above which it is impossible to drive it—so long as it is not induced to plane. It is therefore foolish to try and sail a boat of the latter type faster than its maximum speed and, accordingly, one reduces the sail area and saves the strain on crew and craft—but not so in a

planing dinghy. So we get dinghies over-canvassed on the wind, so
that they may plane faster off the wind ; if someone could design a
really good gadget for reducing and increasing sail area easily in a
dinghy during a race, things would be far more simple.

The technique of sailing a dinghy to windward in strong, gusty
winds, is, therefore, to keep the boat sailing as close to the wind as
possible, but always so that the foresail is properly pulling, except in
rare cases of emergency, and easing the mainsheet to spill the wind
from the main during the heavy puffs. The importance of keeping the
dinghy on an even keel was stressed in previous chapters and it is a
point which no dinghy helmsman can afford to ignore. It may look very
exciting and fine to flog a boat along on her ear, but it is just plain bad
sailing in a dinghy in anything more than a very light wind, and the
correct upright position must be maintained by controlling the amount
of wind used by the trim of the mainsail. This correct control of the
amount of wind used may mean that, in puffy weather, the mainsheet
is constantly being hauled and eased a little, in much the same way as
an angler plays a fish on his line, by first reeling in a little and then
letting his fish run the line out and so on. One does, in fact, often hear
this technique referred to as " playing the mainsail."

It was mentioned in Chapter V that squalls or puffs of wind travelling
at greater speeds than the normal steady wind in which the boat is
sailing, result in the breeze coming a little more free because of the
"apparent wind" effect. In addition to this, of course, the windstream
frequently has to go round buildings, trees, hills and other obstructions,
before it reaches the sails of your boat, and in consequence may be
constant neither in speed nor direction. For these reasons it may be
necessary, when going to windward, frequently to meet changes in the
direction of the wind, both real and apparent, by the alteration of the
course of the dinghy, so that, with the foresail sheeted hard in, a course
is followed that will keep this sail, which is the helmsman's guide in
close-to-the-wind sailing, always just drawing properly. Generally
speaking, the helm should be moved swiftly, sometimes almost jerked,
in order to change the dinghy's course quickly to one on which the
properly trimmed foresail is drawing at its maximum efficiency. It is
no exaggeration to say that, on some waters inland, where there are
many obstructions, the wind may shift in direction by as much as 90°
in a couple of seconds, and under these conditions the helmsman and
crew must be very vigilant to prevent a capsize, especially if they are
sitting well out and going hard to windward when suddenly the wind
slams round and blows on the other side of the sails, threatening to
capsize the boat on top of them. If this situation arises, it is best to
jerk the helm hard towards you, at the same time throwing your weight
over to the other side of the dinghy, possibly pressing down on the far

gunwale with your sheet-hand. If such a slam should hit you on the leeward side of the sails while you are going to windward, it is often wise to tack immediately, to take advantage of the wind shift; but this should not be done if you have reason to suppose that it is a very temporary shift, lasting only a few seconds. This matter really lies outside the scope of the present work, in which no attempt is made to describe racing tactics; but reference to Figure 46 will show the sort of situation in which one might expect a very brief change of wind direction.

We also referred earlier in this book to the manner in which a dinghy is sailed as close to the wind as is possible without "pinching" or upsetting the efficiency of the sails. It was stated that the helmsman should watch an area just aft of the luff of the foresail, which should be sheeted hard in except in very light weather, and sail a course which will keep this part of the sail just full and drawing, bearing away if

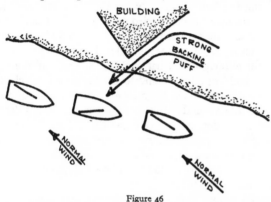

Figure 46

there is any tendency for it to "lift" and, every now and again, luffing towards the wind slightly until the sail just begins to lift and show signs of starvation at the luff; then immediately bearing away again a trifle and keeping the dinghy on that course for a little while—so that the foresail is always just not lifting. In this way the boat will be sailing to the best advantage to windward in moderate or strong winds.

From this and the foregoing paragraphs, it will be gathered that a dinghy cannot be sailed successfully to windward by putting her on a course and keeping her on it, as might be done in the case of many bigger craft. Dinghies are too sensitive for this kind of treatment, and if success is to attend the efforts of a dinghy helmsman he must also develop extreme sensitivity to minute changes in wind strength and direction, smoothing out these differences, as would a good diplomat or liaison officer, before they can affect his craft adversely—carefully picking out and preserving the effects of changes which would benefit the dinghy's progress and eliminating, as far as possible, those changes which would be to its disadvantage.

There is, however, one great danger that arises from this technique; a danger which is all too frequently witnessed, even in the bigger races. It is inclined to produce a tendency towards fiddling with the helm. One sees helmsmen fairly sawing away at their helms for no good purpose at all and merely putting the brake on, for their movements of the tiller are so frequent and rapid that before the boat can possibly be turned at all, the opposite rudder is applied—and so the dreadful process goes on; a pointless waggling which must considerably reduce the speed of the boat.

The tiller of a sailing boat does two main things. Not only is it used to move the rudder and so to guide the boat, but it relays messages from the boat to the helmsman. It is, in fact, a two-way telephone—the helmsman may tell the boat where he wants her to go and the boat may tell the helmsman where she wants him to go. The return wire, from the boat to the helmsman, is rather weak and the latter must be attentive and "holding the line" if he is to get the messages that are sent to him. A few years ago, the writer tried to rig a dinghy with wires to the tiller, from a second tiller amidships, so that she could be steered with the left hand when sitting on either gunwale. The experiment was a complete failure, for although the boat could be steered quite well, it was impossible to "feel" the dinghy and to get the messages which she was trying to send through to the helmsman, because there was too much friction in the blocks and wires connecting the two tillers. Another gadget had to be devised to overcome this difficulty. Now, as far as these messages from your dinghy to you are concerned, it must be pretty obvious that if you are to get the weaker ones, it is not much good holding the tiller in your fist as you would a sledge hammer, but you must handle it with a light touch.

It has been stressed before that a racing dinghy and her human complement aboard are really a team and, as with other teams, it is no use one of the members wanting to do one thing and another wanting to do something else. It is, therefore, nothing short of just plain silly to ignore the desires of your dinghy tugging hard at the helm to go one way, whilst you try to impose your will upon her to make her go in the other direction. Such an unhappy state of affairs must not be allowed to exist and it is useless to grit your teeth and grimly mutter, "Come here, you little so-and-so"; because, if there is any disagreement in the ranks of the team, you will get nowhere very fast. Now you are the master—there must be no doubt about that—and it is up to you to persuade your dinghy to go where you want her to, by making it pleasant and easy for her to do so; everybody will then be happy and content, and as American advertisements would have us believe that contented cows give richer milk, can there be any doubt that contented dinghies will give better speed? So, if your dinghy finds it hard and unpleasant to go in the direction you want her to, find out why. It will nearly always be the question of balance, between the centre of effort of the sails and the centre of lateral resistance, into which we ventured a little in Chapter VI and which was illustrated in Figure 29. If she is always trying to turn up into the wind and so carries weather helm, this means that the C.E. is too far aft of the C.L.R. and the condition can, perhaps, be cured by one or more of four methods whilst you are afloat. The first is to haul the centreplate up a little, thus moving the C.L.R. aft. The second is to haul the foresail in still flatter, whilst the third is to ease the mainsail a bit. (These two methods are really one and the same, for they are only altering the relationship between the trim of the two sails in an effort artificially to move the C.E. further forward.) The fourth method is to move the weight of the crew towards the stern somewhat and so increase the amount of dinghy immersed aft and, at the same time, reduce the amount immersed forward, thereby moving the C.L.R. slightly aft. Generally speaking, it is undesirable to alter the trim of the sails as these should, if possible, be kept at the most efficient angle for the propulsion of the boat ; nor is it advisable to shift the weight of the crew more than a very little, for

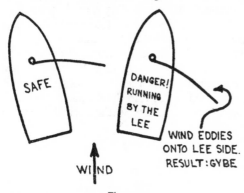

Figure 47

this will upset the underwater shape of the dinghy. It is, therefore, the centreboard that should receive attention. If she still carries excessive weather helm after the centreboard is adjusted as far as is practical, in consideration of its task as a means of preventing leeway, you should, when you can get ashore and re-rig the dinghy, either rake the mast a little further forward or move it further forward altogether. If considerable movement of the mast does not make things better you may have to alter the sail plan.

In heavy weather, running before the wind is probably the most difficult point upon which to steer the boat, especially if the direction of the wind is constantly shifting and threatening to make the dinghy run by the lee (see Figure 47), or gybe all standing, i.e. unawares and uncontrolled! Some of the centreboard should be lowered if the dinghy is inclined to roll badly and it should certainly be at least half way down before a gybe is attempted in strong winds. When gybing, the helmsman and crew should move amidships ; the helmsman then faces aft and shifts the tiller extension towards the side on which it will be needed after the gybe; he then moves the helm up and holds it there with his knee, whilst he hauls a little mainsheet and changes the hand holding it. Directly the sail comes across—which it will do very smartly—he should let the sheet run out a little (the little that was hauled in when the helm was put up), to take the force out of the gybe smoothly, whilst the dinghy should, at the same time, be allowed to luff a trifle, for the same reason. His weight and that of the crew should be shifted to counteract the movement of the weight of the boom and sails and the wind pressure upon them. The dinghy can then be put on her new course and the sails trimmed accordingly.

A point to be guarded against, when planing, is the too forceful use of the helm. At high speeds there is a very "dense" mass of water around the rudder control surfaces and sudden movement may be sufficient to roll the boat right over. It is a case when a pretty firm and steady hand is needed on the helm and your touch will frequently have to be not too light—certainly never too hasty, or you may repent your action while floating alongside your upturned craft.

It is a great mistake ever to turn into the wind faster than you can get your sheets in. For instance, when rounding a mark coming off a run on to a beat on which your sails will be on the same side, do not simply push the helm hard down so that your sails immediately become emptied of wind before you can get them in and trimmed to your new course. Instead, try to sail round the mark, getting the sheets in just as fast as you can, but turning no faster than you can get the sails trimmed. There are occasions when this rule should not be followed, but it is nevertheless a good rule to stick to in the normal course of events.

CHAPTER X

HELMING (3)—POSITIONS AND PREDICAMENTS

*Sitting out—Positions when beating or running—Getting off the mud—
Bent centreplate—What to expect from your dinghy—Sailing limitations
—Safety of others—Assisting a capsized dinghy's crew*

SITTING out probably imposes rather more strain on the helmsman
than it does on the crew, because the latter is to some extent
supported by the pull of the foresail sheets, whereas the helmsman
has the pull of the mainsheet across his body and is therefore not
supported by it. Nevertheless it is, needless to say, just as important
for the helmsman to sit out as it is for the crew, but it will be necessary
for him to see past the crew and he will therefore not be able to lean
quite so far out.

Frequent movement of the helmsman may affect his steering of the
dinghy and the crew should, as far as possible, endeavour to make the
small and numerous moves necessary for the maintenance of the dinghy
in an upright position. Some helmsmen steer from the leeward side in
light weather, but in my opinion it is well-nigh impossible to judge
the trim of the sails from this position. Even when tacking in light
weather, when the helmsman and crew are sitting on opposite sides of
the dinghy, it is preferable that they change sides at every tack. It is
desirable that the skipper sits either on the weather gunwale—if the
crew is also on the weather side—or in the boat on the weather side;
he should not sit in the centre of the boat.

It is obviously wrong for the crew to sit to leeward when beating
in lightish weather, if there is sufficient wind for the helmsman to have
to sit on the weather gunwale to balance him and the wind on the sails,
because this causes unnecessary windage. Off the wind, this does not
matter and before the wind it may be the best position, because, on
this point of sailing, windage is a help rather than a hindrance and
because the foresail can frequently be goosewinged more satisfactorily
from this position. It is hoped that Figure 48 may assist the reader to
understand these remarks.

There is often little blame to attach to a helmsman who runs aground
when racing in strange waters, for it is well-nigh impossible to take
soundings when racing a dinghy, and the only method of determining
the depth of the water is by the sight of the bottom, which may not

always be visible through muddy water even though there be but three or four feet of it. The use of sounding canes or rods is usually forbidden under the racing rules. Frequently, therefore, the first warning that is received of insufficient depth is the sound of the centreplate hitting the bottom or even merely loss of steerage way. Shallow water is, of course, usually marked by buoys and other aids to pilotage, but when racing it is often desirable to get in as shallow water as possible, in order to dodge the full force of an adverse current, and it is at such times that contact with the mud may be made. Though the skipper may not know the exact depth of the water under his dinghy, he should at least know that he is sailing in shallow water and that there is a possibility of hitting the bottom, and he should

RIGHT   WRONG   RIGHT

Figure 48

accordingly, warn the crew of this danger and tell him to keep a look-out for signs of insufficient water and be prepared to raise the centreboard and tend his sheets directly the mud is hit. If this happens when the dinghy is tacking up a shallow shore, it should be possible to avoid more than a momentary contact with the bottom, for directly it is hit the dinghy should be spun round on to the other tack, whilst the crew snatches up the centreboard sufficiently to clear it from the ground, backing the foresail also, if necesary, to blow her head off. If, however, the dinghy is reaching down a lee-shore, it may well be that she gets well and truly stuck and any efforts to relieve the situation by raising the centreplate will merely have the effect of allowing her to be blown sideways into ever shallower water before she gets a chance to gather sufficient way to luff successfully into the channel. Her rudder may eventually ground also and jam on its hangings, so that, if the helmsman goes aft to unship it, his weight depressing the stern merely aggravates the situation. In such circumstances the crew should be ordered overboard immediately and without loss of time; in a 12-*footer* the water will only come up to his chest, or thereabouts, even if the centreboard is right down, though sometimes in *Merlin-Rockets* and *International 14's*, it may come up almost to his neck. Immediately the dinghy is relieved of the weight of the crew, she will probably come clear of the bottom and the crew may be able to haul her round on to the other tack or heading offshore, when she probably will sail off quite easily and he can clamber aboard again. It may be necessary for the skipper to haul up a little more centreboard to free her even after the crew is out of the boat and, if the rudder is stuck, he should move his weight as far forward as possible to release it by raising the stern a little.

If you have the grave misfortune to bend a thin centreplate on the bottom, so that it cannot be raised when you want to bring the dinghy into a shelving shore, perhaps the best thing to do is to lower the sails and paddle her in as far as your jammed centreplate will allow you. Then jump out into the water and capsize her on to her side, without allowing her to fill if possible, and float her, on her side, towards the shore, where it should be easier to remove the centreplate and allow the dinghy to come upright. Figure 49 will give an indication of how this is done.

Figure 49

One of the most useful attributes that a dinghy sailor will acquire in time is the knowledge of what to expect from his boat under all conditions. As a rule a modern racing dinghy will stand up to the most gruelling treatment afloat and, usually, failure to keep sailing under such circumstances arises either from improper handling or the carrying away of defective gear (which really amounts to the same thing, because it is the responsibility of the owner—not the dinghy—to see that worn and inferior gear is replaced with something that will stand up to the demands made upon it). Only very seldom is a dinghy incapable of putting up with the conditions with which her crew is prepared and able to cope.

However, there are naturally limitations on the capabilities of even the best of dinghies and the wise helmsman will accumulate the knowledge of these shortcomings with experience—both his own and other people's—and will sail within the limitations of his boat.

Dinghy racing is very highly competitive and the skill of some of its exponents is great. It would be a mistake for the novice to be so imbued with the competitive spirit as to disregard the limitations both of himself and his boat. Furthermore, as his skill and experience increases, it is his duty not to encourage foolhardiness amongst others of less experience than himself. Accidents do happen when sailing and the daily press invariably gives so much publicity to these misfortunes that perhaps the popularity of small-boat racing suffers accordingly. Most of such accidents could and should be avoided with more care and less unskilled bravado. Certainly mollycoddling either of the boat or her sailors should not be encouraged, any more than should foolhardiness.

It is the duty of everyone who goes afloat, either for pleasure or work, to pay due attention to the safety of others and to be considerate towards them. If it should fall to your lot to have to render assistance to the crew of a capsized dinghy, remember that they may have been sailing hard and be both tired and cold. On no account allow them to reach a state of shivering exhaustion in an effort to right and bail out their boat or get it ashore. The boat is unimportant in comparison with its men and can often be left quite safely until they are ashore and can find a motor boat to take them out to deal with her in safety. If there is no other help available, therefore, do not allow them to reach too tired a state or it may be very difficult to get them aboard your dinghy and, in your struggles to do so, she too may be capsized. Always reduce your sail area by lowering your foresail before taking a rescued crew aboard, for the added weight in your dinghy may impose very severe strains on her hull and rigging. If yours or the capsized dinghy has an anchor, make the line fast to the mainsheet horse of the swamped boat and drop the anchor at the end of the entire length of its line. Even if it does not reach the bottom where you are, it will do so as the dinghy enters shallow water if she is drifting on to a lee-shore. Sometimes, if the capsized boat has plenty of buoyancy apparatus, it may be easy for the crew to right her and sail her home unaided. If this is the case, let them get on with the job unhampered, but keep an eye open to see that all is going well.

CHAPTER XI

MAINTENANCE OF THE HULL

*Specialized nature of maintenance—When and where to work—Interior—
Centreboard slot rubber—Removing the oil film—Rubbing down—The art
of varnishing—Dangers of short cuts—Deep scratches—Preparing to
varnish—Varnishing*

IT is not intended that this and the next chapter shall be anything
more than a guide to the owner on how to maintain his dinghy in
good condition. There is a great deal to be learnt about the care of
a boat whose standard of upkeep is as high and as specialized as that
of the modern racing dinghy; the companion volume to this, "Racing
Dinghy Maintenance," deals with this complicated subject in detail.
No attempt is made here to give anything more than the basic information required to keep the dinghy in a healthy state.

It is often said that a stitch in time saves nine, and never is the truth
of the proverb more obvious than in the matter of dinghy maintenance.
It is not a simple matter to keep in good condition a boat which gets
hard—sometimes even brutal—treatment when she is sailed, even
though the utmost care be lavished upon her when she is not in use.
It demands much hard work. But to *get* a boat into good condition,
once she has been neglected and allowed to deteriorate, may be just
pure drudgery. Even so, if you have to buy a boat in poor condition,
the reward of seeing her well-groomed again will certainly compensate
you for any amount of labour put into her.

Many dinghies are raced all the year through and under these
conditions it is not always easy to choose the best time to carry out the
necessary maintenance work. It should, as far as possible, be fitted in
with your racing programme and it is suggested that the best times for
the work are in midsummer and midwinter or very early spring.
Midwinter is really the better time for doing the complete annual
overhaul than the spring, but the weather is not generally suitable for
the varnishing or painting that may have to be done.

It is not unnatural that some people may grudge a lovely summer
week-end spent fiddling about in a shed ashore with wire, rope and
varnish, when they could be out sailing; but, from a purely practical
point of view, it is an excellent time to do the work. In the first place
it gives one a slight respite from racing, which, though perhaps

unwelcome, may nevertheless be necessary to avoid the danger of getting stale, which may beset some of those who sail a great many races. Secondly, it gives the dinghy a chance to dry out at a time when she can most benefit by it. Thirdly, it is the best and easiest time of year to apply varnish—or would be in a normal climate. Finally, it ensures that the dinghy is on the top line for the most important end-of-season races, which are frequently the biggest of the year.

One of the half-yearly refits should be a very complete overhaul and the other can then be more in the nature of a check-up to ensure that every bit of gear is in good order and to spruce up the surface of the hull somewhat with a light coat of varnish or enamel.

The first thing to do is to choose a place in which to do the work. It should be under cover and where dust will not be disturbed by others, or your newly varnished hull may be spoilt by people brushing against it whilst it is still not properly dry.

Since it will involve a rather more thorough programme, let us consider the jobs to be done in the annual complete overhaul.

Firstly, look to the hull itself. The inside may not require varnishing (or painting) throughout, but there will, almost certainly, be rather heavily worn places which will need building up somewhat, in order that an adequate covering of finishing material may always be present and the bare wood never be exposed. Gunwales, sidebenches, thwarts and floorboards will usually show signs of wear and should, except for floorboards, be kept in as smooth a condition as possible to facilitate the easy movement of the crew when shifting their weight from one place to another. Any patches of bare wood which have been allowed to develop, and the varnish immediately surrounding them, should be rubbed down with Fine Number 2 sandpaper and touched-up or "brought forward" with a little varnish (i.e. bring the level of the bare patch forward to be level with the surrounding varnish). It is a rather messy business, but a finger will be found one of the best things with which to

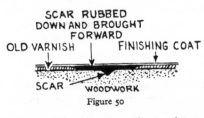

SCAR RUBBED
DOWN AND BROUGHT
FORWARD
OLD VARNISH   FINISHING COAT
SCAR   WOODWORK
Figure 50

apply varnish to small patches, unless a very fine and soft-haired brush can be found. The reason for this is that the edges of the new varnish touching-up must be tapered off over the thinned edges of the varnish around the bare patch (see Figure 50), and this cannot be done with an ordinary varnish brush. The whole of the parts inside which are to be varnished can then be rubbed down after the patches which have been touched-up are dry. Number 0 sandpaper should be used.

The dinghy is now rolled on to her side, on sacks, and tied or propped in that position whilst the centreboard is removed from its casing and the inside of the hull is thoroughly hosed or brushed out to remove the dust of rubbing down and the grit and dirt which are accumulated when sailing. A vacuum cleaner is extremely useful for getting all the dirt out, but it is necessary to wash the boat as well and for this job a stirrup pump is invaluable. After a good swill out and drying off with a chamois leather, the boat will appear considerably refreshed. The gunwales, thwarts and other interior parts which have been rubbed down are not varnished at this stage, as they might be spoilt when the boat is turned upside down, and they are left until after the outside has been done and the dinghy is once more upon her keel. On no account should steel wool be used for rubbing down the inside, as bits of it will break off, get into the boat and be very hard to remove ; if any pieces remain, they will eventually rust and ruin the appearance of the dinghy.

The boat can now be rolled over, bottom upwards. The rubber strip which may be fitted to the bottom of the centreboard case should be inspected and renewed if necessary. A portion of the keel band will have to be removed in order to do this and the new rubber fastened in place with copper tacks, so that the edges of the two rubber strips are just barely touching and the rubber is stretched out a little lengthwise. " Rubber insertion," which has one or more layers of fabric sandwiched between layers of rubber, should be avoided, because the fabric sometimes shrinks when it gets wet and causes wrinkles over the surface. Incidentally, rubber is easier to cut if the knife or razor blade is lubricated with water or, better still, "spit."

Frequently, especially if you sail on water which is used to any extent by power-driven craft, the hull will be found to have a very thin film of dirty oil adhering to it. It may not at first be apparent, but will very quickly clog your sandpaper if it is not removed before you commence to rub down. It should be wiped off with a rag moistened with turpentine. The hull may now be looked over for any scratches and scars. Bad scratches may be rubbed out with Fine Number 2 sandpaper, finished off with Number 0 and touched up with a little varnish. You should not sandpaper away at one spot for too long, for the heat generated by the friction will cause the varnish to peel off instead of being cut down smoothly and it will quickly clog the sandpaper. The very best stuff to use for rubbing down paint and varnish work is Number 320 "Wet-or-Dry" sandpaper—this is a waterproof variety of paper and should be used wet, when it will have a grinding action that produces a far better surface and reduces the labour, as it does not get clogged so easily. Deep scars are best left until after the rubbing down has been completed.

Rubbing down a surface to prepare it for varnish or paint is done for two main reasons. The first is to level off the surface so that succeeding coats will lie smoothly and not in humps and ridges over uneven work below, and the second is to provide a good "keying" surface on to which the new varnish can get a good foothold or grip. Varnish on bare wood will soak in and gain a good hold on it, but, if it is applied directly on to a perfectly smooth and shiny surface, it has nothing to adhere to and may flake off or the surface tension may make it impossible to apply a thin coat over the glossy base, which will not provide the friction necessary to prevent the varnish from breaking up into little globules as soon as it is spread (this latter difficulty is unlikely to be encountered, except in cases where the base is of an exceptionally high gloss). Even though the wood to which the varnish is applied may be perfectly smooth before being covered, the fact that the varnish will soak into the quickly-grown, softer wood to a greater depth than it will into the hard, slow-grown wood, means that the first and second coats will produce ridges over the grain and the work may appear less smooth than it did originally. There is no way of completely avoiding this, but it is a matter really beyond the scope of this book, for we are not much concerned with new work here.

Really good varnishing is an art and is not so simple as might at first be thought. For instance, various surfaces performing different tasks should receive treatment in accordance with the kind of wear which they have to endure. A surface which has to stand up to much hard wear, such as a gunwale over which the weight of the crew is almost continually sliding, should receive a number of thin coats, each one of which should dry out really hard before the next one is applied. The outside of the hull can with advantage be given a thicker coat, which may stand a better chance of giving a perfect surface. Whatever you may hear or read to the contrary, you may rest assured that there is no easy way of getting a first-class surface. There are no short cuts, such as flowing on immensely thick coats or any other method, which can produce results at all comparable to those produced by careful rubbing down and the skilful application of moderately thick coats of varnish. It is always far better to put on a coat that is too thin rather than one that is too thick; for the results of the latter may be a heartbreaking mess of wrinkled runs, which necessitate the tedious and unpleasant toil of scraping the whole lot off and may involve the very real danger of wrecking the base beneath in the effort to put right the horrible state of affairs that has been created by attempting this so-called short cut. Rubbing down reduces the high spots and ridges to the same level as the general surface, whilst succeeding coats of varnish fill in the hollows. The result will be a really smooth flat surface upon which may be applied the final glossing coat. When such a surface as this has been produced, the thin coats of varnish which are required from time to time to keep a good shine on it will only need very light rubbing down, to remove any little highspots which may result from specks of dust having dried into the previous coat.

Although it is hard work with sandpaper, rather than with the varnish brush, which produces a first-class finish, it is nevertheless most important to buy only the best varnish. This must be intended for marine use and it is a very poor policy to attempt to economize by buying a cheap brand. It is not possible for any particular make to be recommended here, but there are two which the writer considers far superior to any other (of about a dozen well-known makes) that he has used and it is his personal opinion that none of the older types of varnish can compete with the best of the new synthetic finishes which are being made today.

Although fine sandpaper is probably the best stuff to use for rubbing down the hull, pumice powder and steel wool can also be utilized if it is only necessary to produce a good keying surface on a perfectly smooth base, and these will be found to be rather less laborious to use. After the hull has been rubbed down, deep scratches that are denting or cutting into the wood may be filled in with marine glue, which may be obtained in white, mahogany and teak colours, or a special "stopper" which is made in mahogany colour only. The former is more plastic when warm and can be smoothed off with a palette or putty knife moistened with turpentine and finally any surplus cleaned off with a turpentiney rag.

The hull is now ready for varnishing and it is a good plan to erect a sheet or old sail over it to prevent specks of dust falling from the roof

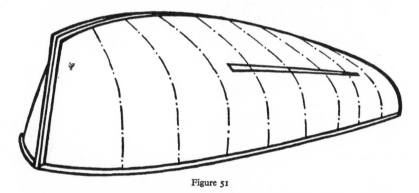

Figure 51

on to a newly finished and wet surface. Never varnish on wet or damp days if you can possibly avoid it. Cold weather makes varnish harder to apply and it will not brush out so easily, but cold will not have such bad effects on the setting of the varnish as will foggy, misty or muggy conditions. Dust off the hull very carefully with a brush and then go over it equally carefully with a wash-leather damped with a little turpentine or mixture of varnish and thinners, taking the utmost possible care to see that every speck of dust is removed. The varnish or paint can then be applied. Clinker-built boats should be varnished plank by plank, starting with the keel and garboard strake and working to the top strake and gunwale, doing one side at a time. Carvel-built boats should be done in strips, as shown in Figure 51. Commencing at the bow or stern, you should varnish along the keel for about 18 inches and then down the hull, to the gunwale, a strip of that width, continuing in the same manner for the whole length of the boat. In this way, no difficulty is encountered when using fairly quick-drying finishes which may harden partially in one place before an adjoining area has been covered, thus making the " joining up " of the two areas hard to accomplish without spoiling that which is no longer fluid.

CHAPTER XII

MAINTENANCE OF SPARS, RIGGING, SAILS AND GEAR

Better sure than sorry—Stretch in new wire—Masts—Booms—Racing flags—Sheets—Toestraps—Kicking straps—Rudders, centreboards and centreplates—Shackles, blocks, winches and sliding goosenecks—Rudder hangings—Keel bands—Sails—Battens—Tillers—Anchor cables

STANDING and running rigging should generally be renewed each year, but this of course depends on its condition. Never, on any account, hang on to rigging " for a little while longer," if it shows the slightest signs of being unfit for its work. The result might be a broken mast, which may be difficult and expensive to replace and may prevent you racing at a time when you most want to do so.

Allow for stretching when you put in new wire rigging. Some types of wire stretch more than others, but generally one can ignore the stretch in the piano wire used for diamond shrouds, and the stretch of halliards and running rigging is not important, as it can be taken up however much there may be. The wire used for shrouds and forestay is that over which most care must be exercised to see that it is not put in too long. If it is arranged so that the rigging screws are just entered by ⅜ inch only into each end of the body when the wire is unstretched, then there will be sufficient adjustment for stretch to be taken up as it occurs. Wire splicing is quite easy when you understand it properly, but unless you already know how to do it, or can spare the time to practise on some old wire with the aid of a good book on how to tackle it, it is better to get it done professionally, for experiments are liable to be expensive. You can cut the wire and seize the thimbles and rigging screws into place at the correct length before handing them over to the rigger. A little grease should be pushed into the bodies of the rigging screws, which will lubricate the threads of the ends as they are screwed home. Sometimes halliards may be turned end for end to prolong their life, but this is not always the result and, once again, it should be emphasized that no risks should be taken with gear the soundness of which you have reason to doubt. New halliards are pulled through hollow masts by making them very securely fast to the old ones ; make absolutely certain that they will not become separated within the mast, for it is no easy matter to get a new wire through if there is nothing to pull it with.

Diamond shrouds should not need any attention in the normal way, but if they are rusty they should be renewed. You should watch out for snags on them on which your sails might get caught or torn; these can be covered up safely with adhesive tape—not insulating tape, as this will make ugly black marks on white sails.

The mast itself may need touching up with varnish, but it should not be necessary to do the whole thing every year. If it does become necessary to varnish the complete mast, rub it down fairly well to ensure that you remove about one coat of varnish from it—in this way it should never be necessary to scrape the mast to remove a great number of accumulated coats which have become thick and heavy. The place where masts get most chafe and wear is the fore side, a little above the deck or thwart, where the foresail sheets rub past when changing tack.

Similar treatment should be received by the boom. This gets chafed against the main shrouds when the sheets are eased on a run and the varnish will frequently have been worn away to the bare wood in this place.

The fabric of the racing flag should be renewed and the pivoting parts of the frame given a little thin oil. If the flag mast is made of aluminium which shows signs of corrosion due to salt water, it can be rubbed off with fine sandpaper and a little Lanolin should then be smeared over it. The Lanolin may be dissolved in cigarette lighter fuel and applied with a brush—it is also excellent for protecting copper and brass from verdigris. The spreaders of diamond rigging may receive similar treatment with advantage.

Foresail sheets will almost certainly have to be renewed twice a year, though a mainsheet may sometimes last two seasons if it is turned end for end after the first year. Fore sheets will show most signs of wear at the place which is in the fairlead when the sail is close-hauled. The round sennit cotton rope, of which sheets are usually made, rots rather easily as it retains a lot of moisture; the mere appearance of the stuff should not necessarily be accepted as a guide to its reliability. It is best to downgrade it to a less important task after two years, as a matter of course.

Another vital item of equipment usually made of treacherous cotton is the toestrap which is responsible for your equilibrium when you are dangling over the weather gunwale in a blow. This usually shows signs of wear first under the centre thwart, where it is commonly clamped by means of a metal plate screwed to the underside of the thwart. Chafe and wear at this place may be very much reduced by padding it on either side with a rubber strip—an old piece from the centreboard slot would do. Anyway, do not allow it any opportunity for treachery, or the result may be a spectacular somersault beneath the waves on some blustery day in the future—a gratuitous subscription from you and your crew to the day's entertainment.

Kicking straps or boom vangs should be renewed as a matter of course, for the job is easy and inexpensive and they take a lot of strain when carrying out their all-important task. Some owners use wire for the kicking strap tackle, but the writer holds that hambro' line is less liable to behead the crew and is more easy to replace.

Rudders and wooden centreboards should receive as careful attention from the varnish brush as does the rest of the hull, for their surface is equally important and they constitute a large proportion of the wetted area of the dinghy, the skin friction of which must be reduced as far as possible. Any nicks in the edges, the protecting strips or tips of these may be smoothed out with a file, or, if they are not protected with a metal edge, the wood may be evened off with a spokeshave. Dents in the lead ballast toes of some wooden centreboards may be tapped out with a light hammer and finished off with an old file or scraper and sandpaper. Metal centreplates should be wiped over with a rag very slightly moistened in thin oil. Any little patches of rust should be removed with emery paper and covered with enamel or wax polish.

Centreboard hoisting tackle should be inspected. The pin on which the centreboard pivots should be removed every other season and checked for wear, being renewed if necessary. Blocks or winches for the tackle should be well lubricated and the tackle itself replaced if it shows any signs of getting tired, for if it should break and allow a half-raised plate to crash down, it might well injure the crew and damage the dinghy. The wire rope from the centreplate to the winch, on those boats provided with them, is very liable to get severely nipped on the winch itself and the galvanizing scratched off it, thus leaving it vulnerable to the attacks of rust.

All shackle pins should be removed and greased, whilst blocks and halliard winches must be carefully lubricated and inspected for wear. The track of sliding goosenecks should be cleaned and lightly greased and a little oil applied to the gooseneck swivel pins, also the mainsheet tang swivel pin at the outboard end of the boom.

Fastenings of the rudder hangings occasionally work loose and enlarge the holes in which they are fixed; larger, stouter screws may have to be used if this has occurred. Keel bands frequently get rather badly worn when the dinghy has to be launched down a stony beach or concrete slipway, and should be renewed before the heads of the screws fastening them to the keel get too badly worn to permit their withdrawal with a screwdriver. It is a good plan, when fixing a new keel band, to countersink the heads of the screws fairly well below the surface and fill in the gap above them with marine glue or even soft solder, which can easily be removed when you wish to withdraw the screws. This will prevent the screw heads becoming worn and will make a smoother surface to the bottom of the keel band.

Sails must be gone over carefully, seam by seam. A sewing machine may be used to repair any that have become unstitched, but care must be taken to ensure that the thread is at the right tension—it is better for it to be too loose, rather than the opposite. The places most liable to chafe are the inboard ends of batten pockets and the luff side of the

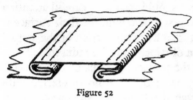

Figure 52

headboard stitching. Small tears can easily be repaired with patches, as shown in Figure 52. It will be seen that the edges of the sail around the hole to be patched are folded back and interlocked between the folded edge of the patch and the patch itself; they are tacked in this position and then sewn with a machine along the outer edge of the patch and the outer edge of the hole. For the sake of clarity, only two edges are shown folded inwards in the figure, but all the edges will be treated in a similar manner.

Although any salt in the sails will have been removed with fresh water after your last sail, they should be soaked in fresh water again for about an hour and then rinsed in several more lots of clean water, after which they should be hung up to dry, being supported every couple of feet from a line, with their luffs fairly taut and horizontal. They should later be stretched for about half an hour in decent weather, before being used for racing.

If your sails have not been setting properly and you think that this is not due to any fault which you yourself can remedy, send them to your sailmaker as early in the autumn as possible with a detailed explanation of the trouble and, if possible, a photograph showing the fault which you wish him to cure. This will allow the repairs or altera-tions to be carried out at a time when the sailmaker is less busy and may mean that you get better work and a smaller bill. Good sails are amongst the best allies that anyone who races a sailing boat can have and they are worth any amount of trouble to get right and keep in good order.

Split battens should be discarded and fresh ones made, care being taken to ensure that suitable wood is used for the job. Mahogany and oak should be avoided as they stain white sails when wet; bakelized fabric and other plastics are sometimes used with success for battens, but the woods commonly used are ash and beech—the former is to be preferred. Never, in any circumstances, use a sail without the battens in it—for there are few ways of more quickly ruining it.

Pull sticks or tiller extensions are apt to wear near the pin which attaches them to the tiller and are liable to break at this point. If there is any sign of a fracture here, fit a new one. "Sloppiness" on the pin can often be remedied by tapping round the edges of the latter with a light ball-headed hammer.

Tillers frequently become loose in rudder heads and it is tempting either to pack them, and so make them fit, or else to ram them further in and drill a new hole for the pin. Either of these methods is to be avoided, because if the boat should capsize and the tiller become thoroughly soaked and swollen the tiller may then jam in position, and this might cause difficulties when she is eventually brought ashore. The best plan, therefore, is to swell the tiller occasionally in a bucket of water and so keep it a snug fit in the rudder head.

The anchor line should not be forgotten and, if normally kept on a reel, should be unwound. It should then be stretched and tested for strength. If you decide that it is fit for further service, it should be soaked in fresh water, coiled down in a large coil and allowed to dry. Clothes line in the form of round sennit is quite good for anchor cable, as it will not kink, but it retains rather a lot of moisture and is liable to rot easily. If stranded rope is used, it should be well stretched, shrunk (in fresh water), and stretched again, to make it easier to handle.

None of these jobs are hard to do and if they are carried out as a normal routine, the arduous tasks or heavy costs of major repairs and replacements should not be encountered.

THE END

JOINING A CLUB

The objects of a sailing club—Advantages of membership—Royal Yachting Association—Applying for club membership—Getting a crewing job—Dinghy sailing clubs—Advantages of the numerically large classes—Open races—Subscriptions and expenses—Sailing journals

IF you want to play a game of football or cricket, you have to gather together two teams, find a suitable field, mow it, mark it out with boundary lines, fix goal posts or stumps and set about finding a referee. Similarly, if you want to have a proper sailing race, you need several boats to race against, a suitable stretch of water, marks to race around, starting and finishing lines and someone to start and time the boats in and settle any queries arising out of the rules as applied to the race.

These are not very deep observations perhaps, but there is a belief in some circles that the function of yacht and sailing clubs is purely social or of snob value; this is quite untrue. The function of any club is to bring together people with the same interests, so that they can follow those interests to the best advantage. Funds are contributed and facilities, on a greater or lesser scale, are provided for the contributors, so that the benefit achieved for all is far greater than that which most individuals could provide for themselves. Quite apart, therefore, from the companionship and social aspects of a sailing or yacht club, there will probably be changing rooms conveniently near to your boat, storage for your gear and possibly your dinghy, perhaps a slipway up which you may haul her and private and protected land on which you may leave her, not to mention the comfort of clubrooms and food when you come ashore and the opportunity to discuss sailing with others. Nor must the convenience of a library and access to yachting periodicals be forgotten.

It must be quite obvious, therefore, that one of the very first things to do if you have decided to take up dinghy racing is to join a suitable club, if you do not already belong to one.

There are sailing clubs on all our coasts and most of our sailable rivers and lakes inland. In choosing the club to which you wish to belong, you will of course consider its geographical position, the ease with which you can reach it and whether it has the facilities which you yourself require. The facilities offered differ from club to club, some of which cater especially for dinghy sailors and their craft. A list of a number of well-known clubs which organize races for dinghies will be found in Appendix II, but this is by no means complete, and a list (price 2s. 6d. post free) of the names and addresses of all yacht clubs in the British Isles can be obtained from the Secretary of the Royal Yachting Association, whose address is 78 Buckingham Gate, London, S.W.1.

The importance of the Royal Yachting Association, usually referred to as the R.Y.A., cannot be too strongly emphasized. This Association is the body responsible for organizing sailing races for all classes of craft throughout the British Isles, and all the yacht or sailing clubs of importance are affiliated to it. In addition to the membership of clubs, there is also a private membership of individuals. Clubs which are recognized and affiliated to the R.Y.A. pay an annual subscription in proportion to their income, so that all members of such a club are, in fact, contributing in some small measure to the finances of the Association. The fact remains, however, that the measure is very small in relation to the benefits which are bestowed upon everyone who races or sails boats, and the Association desires and deserves the support of many more individuals, who have the choice of two forms of membership—either Associate or Full. Associate Members pay an annual subscription of one guinea a year and have no voting power, but receive free copies of the Racing Rules, Fixture Cards and Reports, and are entitled to have their craft registered for half the normal fee, if they are of National or International class—as this fee is normally between twenty and thirty shillings for dinghies, this is quite a consideration. Full Members, at a subscription of two guineas, are entitled to all the Association's publications and are entitled to a vote, whilst the registration of their craft is free.

As an example of the very important work carried out by the R.Y.A., it should be mentioned that it was mainly due to its efforts that the purchase tax on new craft was removed and that the ban on the use of timber for the construction and repair of yachts and boats was made somewhat less rigid under the " hardship scheme," which permitted builders who would otherwise have been put out of business to carry on their work to a limited degree. Over 12,000 letters leave the office of the R.Y.A. every year, dealing with problems from home and overseas, and the value of this activity cannot be over estimated.

It is very likely that you will have a friend who will introduce you to the club of your choice and nominate you for membership. If you are not thus fortunate, you should write to the club Secretary and let him know that you would like to join his club. He will very possibly ask you to visit the club when he is there and this will give you an opportunity to see what it has to offer you and incidentally will give him a chance to see what you have to offer the club. Keenness on sailing and the will to learn to help with the small voluntary jobs that are done in any club should be the key to most sailing clubs. Generally speaking, a club requires that candidates for membership should be nominated and seconded by friends who are already members, but if this is impossible, the rule is often waived. Applications for membership are frequently posted up on the club notice board for some weeks before they go before the committee. On election, the Secretary will inform you and send you a book of rules—your subscription and entrance fee, if any, will then be due.

Even before you become a member, it may be possible for you to get a crewing job and the Secretary may be able to introduce you to somebody who needs a crew. Good crews are often hard to find, but in spite of this shortage of foresheet hands, owners are naturally a little diffident about taking novices afloat with them ; so do not be disheartened if your offer is not jumped at immediately. If it is known that you want to crew, the opportunity will turn up sure enough, sooner or later, and there is certainly no better way of learning to race than to crew for a good helmsman.

Perhaps one of the best ways of speeding up your acceptance as a crew is to make yourself as useful as you can when there are hands needed about the club. There are times when obviously a lift would be welcome when dinghies are being launched or brought ashore or, perhaps, when boats are being manhandled on to racks in the boathouse, or being put on trailers. Willingness to help at such times will not go unnoticed and will probably have its reward in an early offer of a crewing job.

As has already been mentioned, some clubs cater almost exclusively for dinghy sailors and the facilities offered by these clubs are adapted particularly for their needs. Such clubs will probably encourage racing in one or more of the numerically larger classes and the advantage of these classes may here be discussed. The characteristics of these classes have been summarized as far as possible in Chapter I, but the main point which they have in their favour when compared with purely local classes, is that these dinghies can be raced in very many parts of the country against other boats in their own class. This means that if you have a dinghy in any of these classes and have to move to another district, it is not necessary to sell your boat and buy another of the class local to the new area, but you can take your original boat with you and will have the interest and pleasure of seeing how she compares with her new rivals. Furthermore, if you have a car and a trailer you can take your dinghy away to other stretches of water and race there with fresh competition and new interests. There are a number of open races every year for boats in these large classes and to these races dinghies are brought from all over the country and, as most of these represent the best from their district, the winner of such races really has achieved something worth while. This aspect of dinghy racing is most delightful and has something of the charm of cruising in it, for fresh friends are made and old friends met again. This variety of competition and environment is invigorating and makes great demands on the skill of helmsmen, who must be adaptable and understand the fundamental principles governing tidal and stream currents and the effects of features of the land on the wind and not just rely on local knowledge gained over a period of time.

Club subscriptions naturally vary considerably. Those clubs which are mainly concerned with dinghies usually have a rather lower subscription than others. There are sometimes reduced subscriptions for members living more than a certain distance from the club, who are therefore not likely to use it during the week, whilst those under a certain age are frequently admitted as Junior Members at a much reduced subscription. Some clubs also have a sort of family membership scheme under which all the family can become members on paying a special form of "family subscription." Certain clubs, of course, offer far wider facilities than others and subscriptions vary accordingly between about one and five guineas per annum. In addition to the annual subscription, there may be moderate boathouse or mooring rents to pay and small voluntary subscriptions to prize funds or for gratuities to club employees. Boathouse and mooring rents are usually far below those charged by local boatyards and you will frequently be paying for something both safer and more suitable.

Before the close of this book, the desirability of taking a good yachting journal should be mentioned. Dinghy classes are so widespread over the country and developments are so swift that, unless an effort is made to keep up to date, much of the advantage of others' experience may be lost. If you decide to race in open events against strange competitors, you may know much about the performance of your opponents and their boats before the race commences from reports of similar contests, and few things can be of greater value to the racing man than to know exactly what he is up against. Good reporting on dinghy racing should give you much useful information and not just a collection of times and names, and generally afford much arm-chair pleasure.

SAFETY MEASURES

Buoyancy apparatus—Testing buoyancy—Stopping a capsized boat drifting—Life-jackets—Righting the boat—Getting aboard—Bailing out—Assisting others

THE buoyancy apparatus of a racing dinghy has two main functions. The first is the more obvious—to provide lift to a capsized and waterlogged boat and to make her float sufficiently high to support the crew in reasonable safety. The second function is to enable the boat to be easily righted and to help to maintain her in a fair state of equilibrium and stability.

It may at first seem a little strange that these two functions are somewhat conflicting. To get the maximum lift in a waterlogged boat, the buoyancy apparatus should be as low down in the boat as possible, but when thus arranged it may well make the boat difficult to right and to keep righted. Figures 53 and 54 will help to explain why this may be so.

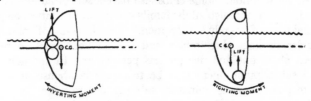

Figure 53   Figure 54

Conversely, the arrangement of buoyancy most conducive to stability may provide comparatively little lift—though it is undoubtedly the safest. The *Cadets*, for instance, have four cylindrical bags fastened in the angle between the deck and the topsides at each end of the cockpit on both sides of the boat, as in Figures 55 and 56, which makes them as safe as houses, even though they

Figure 55

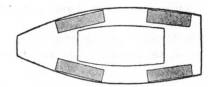

Figure 56

must therefore lie fairly low in the water when swamped. The safest boat is one which, when waterlogged, becomes a stable raft in which the crew can sit—awash maybe—until they are rescued or contrive to get ashore or bail out. Another point in favour of this arrangement is that, with it, the gunwales float comparatively near to the level of the water and make it far easier to scramble back on board again from over the side.

The arrangement that is most suitable for the majority of centreboarders tries to get the best of two worlds. A large buoyancy agent—be it bag, box or tank—in the bow and another large one in the stern provide plenty of lift; side tanks or bags fastened reasonably high up, below the side benches, for instance, provide the stability and help in righting the capsized boat. This arrangement is shown in Figures 57 and 58. Such an arrangement gives maximum fore and aft stability as well as athwartships, and this is equally important—there is no future in a waterlogged boat that floats with her nose in the air, as in Figure 59.

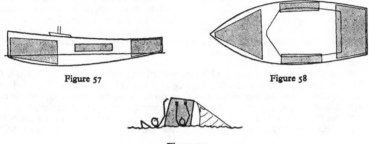

Figure 57   Figure 58

Figure 59

A practical test made by filling the boat full of water and seeing if it will support a substantial weight about amidships for a reasonable time is the only proper way of seeing that the apparatus is in good order. The National and International dinghy class have to do such a test every year, and other classes would do well to make similar rules and conduct similar tests. Or, if there is no organization within the class to make such rules and see that they are carried out, then the clubs responsible for racing these boats should insist on them having sufficient apparatus and seeing that it is tested annually—only then issuing a club buoyancy certificate, without which no centreboarder should be allowed to race in club events.

Not even a straightforward buoyancy test ensures that the apparatus is one hundred per cent. correct. For one thing, a buoyancy bag or tank that seems firmly enough secured when the boat is waterlogged in an upright position, may break adrift if the boat is heeled on to her side. Nor, for that matter, is once a year really often enough for a test, though to do the test more often is scarcely practical. An experienced and observant dinghy sailor can often find defects in the buoyancy arrangements—particularly in the securing of the gear—that might not be revealed in a conventional test. There should, therefore, be a proper annual *inspection* at the same time as the buoyancy test, and quarterly inspections in between.

What it all boils down to is that individuals ought to be sufficiently competent in the art of seamanship to be able to make certain for themselves that their buoyancy gear is efficient. If they don't, they may be not only a nuisance to others but a menace to themselves.

One of the principal dangers is that a capsized boat can drift surprisingly fast, even when waterlogged. Against which must be noted the fact that even a good swimmer makes pretty poor headway when cluttered up with clothing. A dinghy's buoyancy may not always be the whole answer to safety, especially in winter or early season sailing.

The water is probably at its coldest in March. A chap may go out for an early sail after a winter lay-up. Perhaps he wants to do some quiet tuning and so goes single-handed. It is not blowing hard—easy stuff for a summer sail—but it is gusty and his sense of balance and skill is not at the same high pitch as it would be after a few more practice sails. Over he goes, capsized into the icy water. He swallows a mouthful as he goes under. The cold takes his breath away and he gasps as he surfaces just astern of his boat—and swallows the top off a wave in so doing. He's a good swimmer, but he's wearing a lot of clothes and the cold upsets his breathing and reduces his own buoyancy. The boat, floating on her side, perhaps not even swamped, is drifting away down wind and he strikes out after her. She doesn't appear to be drifting fast, but he does not get any nearer to her. She's only got to drift a fraction of a knot faster than he can swim and the consequences are obvious.

What is the answer to that one? There are two. The first is that winter dinghy sailors should wear some form of floatation themselves, to help keep them buoyant when they cannot get their breath in cold water and they are weighed down by clothing. The second is that, since separation from the boat is the first step towards trouble, single-handed helmsmen should make a line fast to the centre thwart of the boat and round their waists, or tie a line on to the end of the mainsheet and round their middles; if you cannot accept the idea of tying yourself to the boat, remember to hang on to the mainsheet like grim death if you go over.

If the dinghy is being sailed with two aboard and one of them gets separated from the boat, which may be floating high on her side and being blown off to leeward faster than he can swim, the chap on the boat can reduce the speed of drift almost to nothing by getting over to leeward and treading on the mast, so as to put the sails well down into the water and make them act as a sea anchor, as in Figure 60. Do not press the mast down so far that the boat is completely

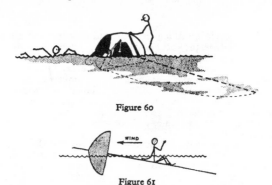

Figure 60

Figure 61

inverted, for then neither you nor the other chap will have much to hang on to. The boat is less likely to invert if the mast is to windward of the hull (Figure 61).

It is better to run the risk of sticking the mast in the mud and breaking it than to let the boat blow away from the crew, but if there is a strong current it may be equally fatal to jam the mast into the bottom, because it may hold her against the current, while the man in the water gets carried away by it. If possible, when trying to stop drift by sinking the sails, get the boat so that she is lying across the current with her mast lying *down-current*; if she is lying with the mast pointing up-current, the stronger current below the surface pressing on the sails and mast may turn her completely upside down. She will also be all right if she lies head or stern on to the current.

It is not uncommon for a crew to somersault backwards out of the boat because of a broken or missed toe-strap. The boat does not always capsize and in a moment she sails out of reach; even though the crew may understand the sailing of her single-handed, the wind is frequently too strong for him to manage the boat and pick up the swimmer quickly. I would suggest—certainly if the dinghy has plenty of buoyancy and there are rescue boats or other craft in the offing, though not necessarily the immediate vicinity—that the dinghy should immediately be allowed to capsize, the crew with her making certain that he hangs on to her as she goes—and the mast pressed down in the water as already described, so that the separated member can catch up with the boat. This advice is offered with some reserve, for it presumes that the man in the water can swim tolerably well and that the dinghy is definitely too much of a handful to manage single-handed.

Most racing dinghies will lie hove-to very well. The boat is luffed almost head to wind and the jib sheeted hard in on the *windward* side, the helm and the mainsheet being left to their own devices; the centreboard must be right down. It is a good idea to practise doing this sometimes with new crews. Hulls with little lateral resistance, such as *Flying Fifteens*, will make rapid leeway, but others lie fairly still and there may be times when lying hove-to may be sufficient to enable the chap in the water to reach the boat. He may find it difficult to climb aboard immediately, and it is better to let him recoup his strength a little before he tries.

It is often possible to right a capsized boat with her sails still up, but if difficulty is experienced, lower the mainsail. Advice on righting the boat is given on pages 73 and 74. The best way of attracting help is to take the main and jib off and then hoist the jib upside down on the main halyard, till the head of the sail comes to the gooseneck; this looks odd and may convey the fact that all is not well with you.

There is a rule under which we all race (R.Y.A. Rule 19 (2)) which says that "All yachts shall render every possible assistance to any vessel or person in peril . . ." etc. The next rule says, "A yacht neglecting to render assistance when in a position to do so shall be disqualified." When there are ample rescue boats about, maybe the obligation to look to the safety of other competitors is relieved, but the rule is there and there seem to be occasions sometimes when it is not observed. Perhaps I am wrong—let's hope I am. It may be extremely difficult to judge when a boat or a person is in peril, but if there is any doubt, the correct action is obvious.

The most effective safety measure is the wearing of some form of life-jacket. There are now special inflator jackets made for dinghy sailing. Rescue boats are a help and a comfort to worried race officers, but they may be of limited use when there are more than half a dozen boats racing. One boat may go over on a reach and take the launch five minutes to see to her safety, by which time the other boats are three quarters of a mile away—and so it goes on. Under certain circumstances and if there are enough of them, launches may be the complete answer, but very often they are inadequate for the tasks they might have to perform.

SOME OF THE MANY CLUBS GIVING REGULAR RACES FOR DINGHIES

LONDON AREA
Putney:
  Ranelagh Sailing Club
Twickenham:
  Twickenham Yacht Club
Teddington:
  Tamesis Club
Kingston:
  Minima Yacht Club
Hampton:
  Hampton Sailing Club
Surbiton:
  Thames Sailing Club
Aldenham:
  Aldenham Sailing Club
Broxbourne:
  Broxbourne Sailing Club

UPPER THAMES
Abingdon:
  Abbey Sailing Club
Henley:
  Henley Sailing Club
Bourne End:
  Upper Thames Sailing Club
Cookham:
  Cookham Reach Sailing Club
Staines:
  Staines Sailing Club
Weybridge:
  Desborough Sailing Club

SOUTH COAST
Hayling Island:
  Hayling Island Sailing Club
Itchenor:
  Itchenor Sailing Club
Dell Quay:
  Dell Quay Sailing Club
Bosham:
  Bosham Sailing Club
Hamble:
  Hamble River Sailing Club
Mengeham Rithe:
  Mengeham Rithe Sailing Club
Fareham (winter only):
  Fareham Motor Boat and
  Sailing Club
Lymington:
  Royal Lymington Yachting
  Club

Portsmouth:
  Portsmouth Sailing Club
Langston Harbour:
  Langston Sailing Club
Hill Head:
  Hill Head Sailing Club
Stokes Bay:
  Stokes Bay Sailing Club

SOUTH WEST
Looe:
  Looe Sailing Club
Coombe Cellars:
  Shaldon Sailing Club
Teignmouth:
  Teign Corinthian Yacht Club
Exmouth:
  Exe Sailing Club
Salcombe:
  Salcombe Yacht and Sailing
  Clubs
Babbacombe:
  Babbacombe Sailing Club
Torquay:
  Torquay Corinthian Yacht Club

WEST
Cheddar:
  Bristol Corinthian Yacht Club
Clevedon:
  Clevedon Sailing Club
Weston-super-Mare:
  Weston Bay Yacht Club
Tewkesbury:
  Avon Sailing Club

SOUTH EAST
Whitstable:
  Whitstable Yacht Club
Herne Bay:
  Herne Bay Sailing Club

EAST ANGLIA
King's Lynn:
  Ouse Amateur Sailing Club
Wroxham Broad:
  Norfolk Broads Yacht Club
Blakeney:
  Blakeney Sailing Club
Snettisham:
  Snettisham Beach Sailing Club

Hunstanton:
  Hunstanton Sailing Club
Brancaster:
  Brancaster Staithe Sailing Club
Wells:
  Wells Sailing Club
Wolverstone:
  Royal Harwich Yacht Club
Aldeburgh:
  Aldeburgh Yacht Club
Peterborough:
  Peterborough Yacht Club
Ely:
  Ely Sailing Club
Waterbeach:
  Cam Sailing Club

MIDLANDS

Farndon:
  Trent Sailing Club
Long Eaton:
  Trent Valley Sailing Club
Burton-on-Trent:
  Burton Sailing Club

Thrapston:
  Middle Nene Cruising Club
Beeston:
  Beeston Sailing Club

NORTH EAST

Cleethorpes:
  Cleethorpes Sailing Club
Tynemouth:
  Tynemouth Sailing Club
Middlesbrough:
  Tees Yacht Club
Hornsea Mere:
  Hornsea Sailing Club
Naburn:
  Yorkshire Ouse Sailing Club

SCOTLAND

Dundee:
  R.N.S.A. Tay
Granton:
  Royal Forth Yacht Club
Granton:
  Almond Yacht Club

A full list of the Sailing and Yacht Clubs affiliated to the Royal Yachting Association is obtainable from the Secretary, 78 Buckingham Gate, London, S.W.1. There are almost five hundred clubs in the R. Y.A. list, which also contains the names and addresses of the Club Secretaries.

INDEX

Accidents, avoidance of, 100
Advice on choice of boat, 10
Alterations to sails, 110
Anchor, 38
    cable, 38
    cable drum, 75, 81
    line, maintenance of, 111
Anchoring, 75
Apparent wind, 52, 92
Assisting other boats, 100
Attaching towline, 74, 75
Avoiding accidents, 100

Backing foresail, 42, 43
Bailer, 38
Bailing, 73
Battens, maintenance of, 110
    plastic, 110
    sail, 34
Beating, 50
Bent centreplates, 99
Boathouses, club, 115
Boom, attaching sail to, 34
    vang, 66, 67, 109
Buoy, securing to, 45
Buoyancy apparatus, 116-118
    inflation, 39
    personal, 118, 119
    test, 117
Buying a boat, 24
    new boat, 27
    second-hand, 26, 27, 28, 29

Cadet, 10, 19, 20, 24, 25, 26, 30
Capsize Drill, 118, 119
    righting, 119
Capsizing, 73, 74
Centre of effort, 64, 95
    lateral resistance, 63, 64, 95
Centreboard adjustment, 63, 64, 95
    function, 63
    hoists, 39
    hoist, maintenance of, 109
    installing, 77, 78
    maintenance of, 109
Centreboard slot rubber, 103
Centreplates, bent, 99
Certificate of measurement, 29
Changing tack, 90
Chinese gybe, 66
Choice of boat, advice on, 10
Class, choice of, 24
Classes, local, 9, 10, 23
    new, 10, 22, 23
Class rules, 27

Cleaning hull, 103
Clothes, 31, 32
Club boathouses, 115
Clubs giving dinghy races, 120, 121
    how to join, 112, 113, 114
    importance of, 112
    subscriptions, 115
Coming ashore, 83, 84, 99
Cost of maintenance, 25
    mast, 25
    sails, 25
Course, sketch of, 82
    studying, 39
Crew, importance of, 31
Crew's obedience, 75
    position, 60-63, 97
    position tacking, 58, 59
Crewing, Chapters III, IV, V, VI, VII
Curve of sails, 53, 54

Dark glasses, 32
Dinghy racing clubs, 120, 121

Easing sheets, 91
Equilibrium, maintenance of, 60, 90
Equipment required for dinghy, 30

Family sailing, 20, 22, 26
Feeling the helm, 94
Figure of eight knot, 34, 37
Firefly, 10, 15, 24, 25, 26, 27, 30
Five-O-Five, 22, 23
Fixing rudder, 42, 83
Fleetwind, 11, 22
Foot, mainsail, 80
Fore and aft trim, 38, 62
Foresail, backing, 42, 43
    goosewinging, 56
    halliard, 33
    hoisting, 33
    lowering, 43
    sheets, 34
    sheets, maintenance, 108
    stick, 82
    trimming, 54, 55
    trimming in puffs, 56

Gear limitations, 100
Glasses, dark, 32
Goggles, 32
Going afloat, 83
Gooseneck, 38
    downhaul, 72
Goosewinging foresail, 56
G.P. 14's, 11, 21
Graduate, 11, 21, 22

INDEX

Gusts, 90, 91
  change of wind direction, 53
Gybe, Chinese, 66
Gybing, 95, 96
  spinnaker, 57

Halliard, foresail, 33
  winches, 37
Handling masts, 78, 79
Hauling the mainsheet, 89
Headgear, 32
Heaving-to, 119
Heavy weather sailing, 68
Heeling, disadvantages of, 60
  prevention of, 60, 61, 90, 91
Helm balance, 94, 95
  feel of, 94
Helmsman's position, 89, 97
Hornet, 10, 19
Hosing down, 46
Hull, cleaning out, 103
  condition, 27-29
  hosing down, 46
  maintenance, 102-106

Inserting kicking strap, 67
Insurance, 25
International 14, 10, 13, 14, 25, 26, 30
International Yacht Racing Union, 11

Jib, see Foresail
  stick, 56, 82
Joining a club, 112, 113, 114
Jollyboat, 23

Keel bands, maintenance, 109
Kestrel, 22
Kicking strap, 66, 67, 86, 109
  attachment, 38
  fitting, 67
  inserting, 67
Knots, figure of eight, 34
  for sail battens, 37
  in foresail sheet, 34
  in mainsheet, 37
  overhand, 34
  stopper, 34

Landing, 43
Lanyards, 33
Launching, 42, 83
  trollies, 41, 45
Leaving the shore, 42, 83
Leech lines, 81
Leeway, 51, 60, 61, 63, 64, 65
Lifting a dinghy, 41
Light wind trim, 62
Limitations of gear, 100
Local classes, 9, 10, 23
Look-out, 66

Lowering foresail, 43
  mainsail, 43, 45
Luff mainsail, 80
Luffing, 91

Magazines, yachting, 115
Mainsail foot, 80
  hoisting, 34-38
  lowering, 43, 45
  luff, 80
  trimming, 86, 89-91
Mainsheet attachment, 37
  coiling down, 46
  hauling, 89
  lead, 89
  trim, 92
Maintenance, 101-111
  cost of, 25
  of anchor line, 111
  battens, 110
  blocks, 109
  centreboard, 109
  centreboard hoist, 109
  diamond shrouds, 108
  foresail sheets, 108
  goosenecks, 109
  keel bands, 109
  kicking strap, 109
  racing flag, 108
  rudder, 109
  running rigging, 107
  sails, 110
  shackles, 109
  standing rigging, 107
  tillers, 111
  tiller extensions, 110
  toestraps, 108
  when to do, 101
Making towline fast, 74
Mast, cost of, 25
  deck stepped, 80
  handling, 78, 79
  keel stepped, 79
  position, 95
  rake, 95
  setting up, 32, 33
  stepping, 78, 79
Measurement certificate, 29
Measurers, official, 29
Merlin-Rocket, 10, 15, 16, 25, 26, 27, 30
Moorings, 10, 11, 25, 84
  picking up, 44

National 12, 10, 11, 12, 13, 24, 25, 26, 27, 30
National 18, 10, 21, 25, 26, 30
New boat, buying, 27
New classes, 10, 22, 23

Obedience of crews, 75
Official measurers, 29

One-design classes, 11
Osprey, 23
Overhand knot, 34
Overhauling gear, 102

Paddle, 38
Parts of boat, 2
Patching sails, 110
Personal buoyancy, 118, 119
Pinching, 93
Planing, 71, 91, 96
Picking up a buoy, 84
mooring, 44
Plastic battens, 110
Points of sailing, 49
Port tack, 50
Portability, 26
Position, the helmsman's, 89
Prevention of heeling, 60, 61, 90, 91
Psychology of crew, 76
helmsman, 48
Pumps, 73

Racing flag, 33, 39, 52, 56, 81, 108
Rake of mast, 95
Reaching, 50
Reducing sail, 71, 72
Redwings, 11, 21
Reef points, 72
Reefing, 71, 72, 91
winches, 72
Rendering assistance, 119
Restricted classes, 11
Rinsing sails, 45, 110
Rigging boat, 32-40
screws, 32, 33
state of, 28
Righting a capsize, 73, 74, 119
Royal Yachting Association, 11, 113
Rubbing down, 102, 103, 105
Rudder, fixing, 42
hangings, 109
maintenance of, 109
shipping, 83
Rules, class, 27
Running, 50, 95
aground, 97, 98
in strong wind, 71
rigging, maintenance of, 107

Safety measures, 116-119
of others, 100
Sailing ashore, 43
in heavy weather, 68-74
to windward, 51, 92, 93
Sail, alterations to, 110
battens, 34
cost of, 25
curve of, 53, 54
maintenance of, 110

Sail patching, 110
reducing, 71, 72
rinsing, 45, 110
sheeting, 50
suction effect, 53, 54
tensioning, 80
trimming, 48-59
Salvage, 100
Seats, sliding, 59
Seaworthiness, 26
Second-hand buying, 26, 27, 28, 29
Securing to buoy, 45
Setting spinnakers, 57, 58
Sewing sails, 110
Shallows, 97, 98
Sheets, easing in squalls, 91
foresail, 34
Sheeting sails, 50
Shipping the rudder, 83
Shoes, 31, 32
Shrouds, diamond, 108
Sitting out, 60, 61, 97
Sliding gooseneck, 72
seats, 59
Sounding, 97, 98
Spilling wind, 91
Spinnaker bag, 82
gybing, 57
rigging, 39
setting, 57, 58
stowage, 39
Splice, wire rope, 107
Sponging, 73
Squalls, 68
Standing rigging, maintenance of, 107
Starboard tack, 50
Start, timing, 40
Steering technique, 92
to windward, 53, 55
Stepping masts, 78, 79
Sternway, 68
Stopper knots, 34
Storage, 25, 28
Stowage during racing, 38
Stowing the boat, 46
Stretch in wire rope, 107
Subscriptions, club, 115
Suction effect of sails, 53, 54
Surveying, 27, 28
Swordfish, 10, 20, 25, 26, 27, 30

Tacking, 49, 50, 58, 90
Teamwork, 94
Tensioning sails, 80
Toestraps, 108
Towing, 74
Towline attachment, 74, 75
Tiller extension, 89
extensions, maintenance of, 110
maintenance of, 111

Timing the start, 40
Trailing, 114
Trapezes, 59
Trim, fore and aft, 38, 62
Trim in light winds, 62
Trimming the foresail, 54, 55, 56
     mainsail, 86, 89-91
     sails, 48-59
Trollies, 41
Turning, 90
Turning into wind, 96

What to wear, 31, 32
Winches, reefing, 72
Wind shifts, 92
     turning into, 96
Windward, sailing to, 50, 51, 92, 93
Windward steering, 92, 93
Wire rope splice, 107
     stretch, 107

Yachting magazines, 115